Contents

- an individual (or group) wishing to save a redundant building, or

- a local authority wishing to solve a problem.

But no matter what the starting point, the outcome of this stage has to be a viable scheme (and one which, if possible, is exciting so as to help arouse interest and overcome inertia and scepticism). The case studies and other research show that the important factors for success are:

(1) Uses Matched to Building
(2) Local Authority Support
(3) Viable and Exciting Scheme.

(1) Uses matched to building

Do not waste time and effort on buildings that are basically unsuitable for conversion (see Chapter 3). A great deal of information about a building, and often enough to decide not to pursue it further, can be gathered from just looking at the outside of the building.

- Use a simple worksheet like the Windscreen Survey (Table 4) to give each building a score. Do not waste time on those where the minuses outweigh the pluses.

- In several case studies the project initiator 'knew that the building was right' after visiting it once (Case Studies 1, 3, 4, 5, 10).

- Size is important as it affects the economics of management and hence the sustainability of the end-use. Where full-time management is required, a scheme needs to have an income in excess of £100,000 unless some means of sharing the cost can be found (Case Studies 13, 14).

- Conversion of buildings in poor structural condition, especially if they are listed, should only be undertaken if sufficient funds are in fact behind the project (Case Studies 2, 6, 11). Most of the case

Table 3: Stages in the conversion process

Some Input and Tasks	Key Factors for Success
	● **INCUBATION STAGE**
–Visualise the Potential Uses –Understand Demand –Select the Building –Obtain Local Authority Support –Make Survey and Costings –Formulate the Scheme –Obtain Public Support	● USES MATCHED TO BUILDING ● SUPPORTIVE LOCAL AUTHORITY ● VIABLE AND EXCITING SCHEME
	● **NEGOTIATION STAGE**
–Negotiate Building Purchase –Obtain Planning Permission –Find Appropriate Professionals –Raise the Finance –Maintain Flexibility –Make Detailed Designs –Obtain Quotations –Select Reliable Contractor	● GOOD PROPERTY TERMS ● FLEXIBLE FINANCIAL PACKAGE ● SOUND PROFESSIONAL TEAM ● RELIABLE CONTRACTOR
	● **CONSTRUCTION STAGE**
–Manage the Building Work –Keep Control of Money –Keep Control of Time –Use an MSC Workforce –Deal with the Unexpected	● EFFICIENT PROJECT MANAGEMENT ● FLEXIBILITY WHEN NECESSARY
	● **MANAGEMENT STAGE**
–Market the Scheme –Attract Tenants –Organise Continuing Management –Create Atmosphere of Success –Plan Further Action	● COMMUNICATING THE EXCITEMENT ● MANAGEMENT COMMITTED TO SUCCESS

1　What this handbook is about

Background and Purpose

Converting old industrial buildings has suddenly become quite commonplace. Just as it was realised a few years ago that rehabilitating old houses was usually preferable to pulling them down and building new ones, so it is now acceptable to think of re-using old industrial and commercial buildings. And there is no shortage of large old buildings which are no longer needed for their original purpose, especially in our older industrial towns and cities. Often they have far more character than anything we would build nowadays, and if they are just left empty they soon decay and blight the whole area around them. Often, too, it is cheaper to adapt an existing building than to build a new one, although there may be more problems to overcome. In the past few years, therefore, there has been growing interest in the conversion and re-use of old buildings not only among those who wish to conserve our heritage, but also among those who wish to bring economic life back into run-down areas or just to carry out their own innovative projects. 'Adaptive re-use', as it is sometimes called, is now seen to have an important part to play in urban regeneration.

By now a lot of experience has been accumulated, and the Department of the Environment (DoE), which has supported many conversion schemes through the Urban Programme (UP) and other measures, wishes to publicise successful schemes and to explain how they were devised and organised. The purpose of this is not only to give praise to the pioneers who richly deserve it, but also to provide practical insight and guidance to those who might be involved in future schemes, especially if they are newcomers.

The important thing is to learn from the successes (and failures) of others, and there is now a great deal of success to learn from. This handbook, written by URBED (Urban and Economic Development) Ltd., explains what is involved in devising and implementing a successful re-use scheme and provides practical information, concentrating on the organisational and managerial aspects rather than on technical or architectural matters.

How the handbook is organised

The handbook is written in two parts. The first part contains

- a description of the re-use movement in Britain

   how it has developed
   what future trends might be

- an explanation of the conversion process

- a guide to good practices in organising and managing schemes for the conversion and re-use of industrial and commercial buildings.

The second part contains 14 case studies describing how different organisations from the public, private and voluntary sectors carried out successful conversion schemes in many different circumstances.

These two parts can be read separately or together. Even though there are cross-references, each is designed to make sense by itself. Indeed each case study can be read on its own.

Additional information is given in the appendices. There is a short bibliography in Appendix A. Appendix B contains some statistics on conversions of 400 industrial and commercial buildings, and, while every effort has been made to avoid jargon, some possibly unfamiliar terms do appear in the case studies and are explained in Appendix C.

Selection of case studies

The case studies have been chosen from the long and growing list of successfully completed conversion schemes. In selecting them, care was taken to reflect the great diversity in:

- types of original building

- new uses

- initiating bodies

- sources of finance

- geographical location

so that people undertaking new schemes might be able to find some factors that approximate to their own situation. Broadly speaking the case studies have been grouped into those where the new use is basically workspace (Case Studies 1–5), leisure/retail (Case Studies 6–8), housing (Case Studies 9–10) or mixed use (Case Studies 11–14). Table 1 summarises their general characteristics.

The cases which have been chosen are among those that are generally considered to have been successful or particularly interesting, and are ones which might very well be replicated elsewhere. Very large or special schemes such as Liverpool's Albert Dock or developments by BSC (Industry) Ltd., an offshoot of the British Steel Corporation, have not been included, and managed workspace schemes are covered more fully in Annabel Jackson's *Managing Workspaces* (1). Even so, there are of course many other examples of successful schemes which might equally well have been included.

Each case study is based on a visit to the scheme and interviews with the various parties concerned, as well as on published information. URBED is extremely grateful to all those who have contributed. Their names are listed in Appendix E.

Who the handbook is for

This handbook is primarily intended for:

- those who are planning, or considering undertaking, a conversion scheme and who do not have previous experience of property development

- those, particularly in local authorities, who wish to encourage or appraise such schemes.

It is also hoped that the case studies will be of interest to those who support the idea of regenerating rundown industrial areas and who wish to know more of the efforts which a very wide range of individuals and organisations are now making.

Table 1: Case study characteristics

Case study, location	Original building	New use	Initiating body	Financing
1 Argent Centre, Birmingham	Factory	Small Units	Industrial Association	Private/UDG
2 Curzon Street, Birmingham	Railway Station	Training HQ.	Local Authority	UP/MSC/LA
3 Dean Clough, Halifax	Textile Mill	Small Firms Ind. Estate	Individual	Private
4 Imperial Studios, London	Garage	Hi-Tech Units	Property Developers	Private/UP
5 Mantra House, Bradford	Factory	Small Units	Local Authority	UP/LA
6 The Briggait, Glasgow	Covered Market	Speciality Retail	Conservation Trust	Private/LEG-UP LA/HBC
7 Waterfront Hotel, Hull	Warehouses	Hotel	Individual	Private/HBC
8 Watershed, Bristol	Warehouses	Media Centre + Retail	Development Company	Private/ Sponsors
9 Granby House, Manchester	Warehouse	Housing for Sale	Housing Association	Private/UDG
10 Pipers Ct., Ipswich	Factory	Housing for Rent	Entrepreneur – Builder	Private/ Imp. Grant
11 Bradbury Street, London	Row of Shops	Shops + Offices	Development Agency	UP
12 Camden Lock, London	Stables	Mixed (Inc. Market)	Individuals	Private
13 Canal Museum, Nottingham	Warehouse	Museum + Pub/Restrnt.	Local Authority	UP/Private
14 Pallion, Sunderland	Post War Factory	Community/ Work Centre	Residents' Association	UP/MSC

2

2 The re-use movement

The process of converting a building from one use to another is not new. It used to be the normal practice to adapt buildings for different purposes over their lives. It is only since the Industrial Revolution that it has become common to demolish and rebuild rather than to adapt and extend, and it is only in the past fifteen or twenty years that a movement has grown up in Britain around the idea of conserving redundant industrial and commercial buildings and putting them to new uses. While it is most obvious in the conversion of former large factories and warehouses into small units, the movement now embraces the re-use of buildings as diverse as market buildings and railway stations for a wide range of uses, including housing and specialist retailing. However, these developments are still far from universal, with ideas that have been piloted in London (and perhaps before that in the USA) taking five or ten years to become applied elsewhere. It is also the case that many of the people involved with old buildings are not familiar with the full 'menu' of possible uses and the conditions under which they can work. As a consequence, fine buildings still go to waste because of the failure to devise appropriate schemes or financial packages.

The changing case for conservation

The arguments in favour of the conversion and re-use of old buildings have changed considerably over the past twenty years. In the climate of economic expansion in the 1960's, dominated by large scale urban renewal projects, it was common to regard all but the most venerable buildings as obsolete and that their replacement was necessary in the interests of efficiency and modernisation. This started a growth in concern, voiced by the Civic Trust and others, to preserve fine examples of different architectural styles and stop their replacement with non-descript buildings. At one time the priority was saving country houses, but in the 1970's a new emphasis was put on conserving the traditional character of urban areas and the diverse activities they contained. Technological change, particularly in traditional manufacturing industries, the railways, the docks, and markets, was making some fine buildings redundant. There was also a realisation that many ordinary industrial buildings had a functional character that gave them beauty and distinction (2).

With investment capital becoming harder to attract, it came more and more to be recognised that the stock of existing buildings was an asset which could potentially be used to help revive the economies of run-down urban areas. Indeed in many areas the buildings were worth far more than the land they stood on, and were unlikely to be replaced by new buildings if they were demolished. As a result interest began to shift from finding public uses for old buildings such as museums and galleries, to more commercial uses. This new case was put forward in reports such as *Preservation Pays* (3) by SAVE, which had formerly concentrated on drawing attention to the architectural merit of threatened buildings. It was then shown by such pioneers as David Rock, Mike Franks and Michael Murray that large buildings which were unlikely ever to attract single users again could be converted into satisfactory workspace for small firms. 5 Dryden Street demonstrated that there was a demand for fully serviced workspace from design conscious users, and Clerkenwell Workshops showed that cheap space was just as popular. Thus in the late 1970's economic arguments for conserving old buildings became dominant and gave a new momentum to the re-use movement, spurred on by the general fall in property values coupled with a sharp increase in building costs.

There were still, however, problems in attracting private finance on the scale required. Following the secondary property market collapse of the mid 1970's, bank lending for property developments was restricted. The institutions which controlled the bulk of property investment finance were not interested in schemes that presented complications, and the

(2) Supportive local authority

Local authorities nearly always play an important role in conversion schemes either directly through financial support or indirectly through the need for planning or other permissions. Many schemes are undertaken directly by local authorities themselves, but in other cases they will certainly be the planning authority (although planning permission is not always required) and if Urban Programme or Urban Development Grant funding is to be sought they will not only have to endorse the scheme and submit it to the Department of the Environment for approval, but also to pay one quarter of any grant. Beyond that, all local authorities are concerned about economic decline and about empty industrial and commercial buildings.

In most areas, and in all main towns and cities, there are now local authority officers whose job it is to encourage renewal and revitalisation. They can usually be found in the Planning Department or the Economic Development Department. They will be interested in helping conversion schemes wherever possible, and they can be extremely helpful (Case Studies 1, 2, 4, 6, 10, 11, 14), in some cases virtually joining the development team. For certain types of scheme, such as housing, it may be necessary to seek support from other relevant departments as well. In only two of the case studies (Case Studies 7, 12) were relations with the local authority poor and in neither case have the organisers of those schemes been able to capitalise upon their obvious success by undertaking further schemes in the same area.

> 'We have fought unnecessary battles and got on the wrong side of the Council which we could have avoided . . . If it wasn't for that we could have expanded'

- When a conversion scheme is beginning to take shape seek out allies in the local authority. They can be very useful.

- Local authorities have a lot of knowledge and information on property matters and on what is happening in the area.

- Always contact the planning department, as well as any others, as planning permission is almost certain to be required on a re-use scheme. Even if it is not required it is essential to have this officially confirmed.

- Contact the local authority early if you are interested in an Urban Programme or other grant. They can advise you about the type of schemes which are likely to get support, who to lobby and when to get the paperwork in.

- Satisfying the Building Regulations and Fire Regulations can add dramatically to the cost of conversions, and sometimes make them uneconomic. It is essential to be familiar with the main requirements for a particular scheme and to understand their cost

implications. The local authority will know who should be consulted.

- When the stage of making formal applications for statutory permissions is reached, local authorities usually expect schemes to be presented by an architect, so involve your professional advisers before then.

(3) Viable and exciting scheme

The end product of the Incubation Stage must be a viable and, if possible, exciting scheme. It must at least excite the driving force. If not, the necessary effort and commitment will not be forthcoming and in the end there will be nothing positive to attract potential customers. The scheme must also be viable especially in the long term, so that it is sustainable, and stands a reasonable chance of obtaining the resources needed to get it off the ground.

- If the scheme is not viable or does not have a driving force who understands the development approach required and is capable of, and committed to, taking the scheme through to sustainable success, then shelve it.

- The classic way of deciding whether a project is viable is by doing a written Feasibility Study or Business Plan, describing

>   Objectives
>   Markets (for proposed end-uses)
>   Organisation (people to run the scheme)
>   Operations (how the scheme will work)
>   Revenues
>   Costs (including building costs)
>   Anticipated Funding
>   Evaluation (financial and other).

- This should be passed on as as much factual information as possible, and provided by recognised professionals wherever possible. But the fact is that many successful entrepreneurs do not make Feasibility Studies even when they could well afford to. Those running three of the four privately financed schemes described in the case studies laughed openly at the thought of preparing a detailed Feasibility Study. One managed to produce the back of an envelope with calculations on it; another said that the most they ever did was to prepare a single page financial appraisal.

- Feasibility Studies can serve two purposes:-

>   to help those originating a scheme decide whether or not to go ahead with it
>
>   to convince outsiders that they should support the scheme, usually financially.

Those that are produced nearly always have the second purpose in mind, whereas during the Incubation Stage it is the first purpose that is relevant.

Important

whoever is managing the contract to foresee problems and overcome or avoid them. Useful advice is given in the DoE's *Control of Capital Projects* (20).

- If fixed price contracts have been negotiated, the penalties for failing to manage the project efficiently will fall in the first instance on the contractor.

- Where the developer is bearing the costs of variations from an agreed specification of bill of quantities (which is the case under the Standard or Joint Contracts Tribunal (JCT) contract), effective supervision of the work is essential. This can be supported, but not substituted for, by efficient monitoring against the specification (which in effect becomes the detailed budget).

- In most cases the architect or the driving force were able to supervise the contractors perfectly adequately, but many paid tribute to the role of the quantity surveyor. Clear responsibilities are needed on a construction site. Make sure that you are going through the agreed channels of communication.

- Simple control procedures seem to be perfectly adequate, for example:–

  Time Schedule (Bar Chart). A diagram showing when each main item of work is due to begin and end, which the contractor updates regularly. The quantity surveyor also checks progress against this. It is important that everyone is working off the same document and that progress is reviewed against it regularly. Delays in completing the contract almost always lead to higher costs plus delays in future income. Insist on explanation of, and clear plans to deal with, any significant slippage.

  Budget. The quantity surveyor uses his original detailed estimate of the work and its cost (the Bill of Quantities) as a budget against which to check the rate of expenditure. If he sees costs unavoidably over-running in one area a skilled quantity surveyor is often able to suggest cut backs in other areas to try to keep the total cost within limits.

  'It is not just the major unexpected things that can hit you. It is all the little things that add up unnoticed unless someone is out there spotting them'

  Cash Flow. Someone must watch how the cash inflows and the cash outflows are balancing out. This is the ultimate score card for survival.

- Changes to agreed specifications are liable to be expensive. Try to think things through in advance. That is what the professional developers do (Case Studies 4, 9).

- Where a professional Project Manager is appointed (Case Studies 5, 6, 9) there is always potential for conflict with the driving force. The use of an outside Project Manager would seem to be more suited to the conventional development approach, whereas the driving force will be more directly involved under the entrepreneurial approach.

(9) Flexibility when necessary

Old buildings are notorious for producing unexpected problems. And it is not just construction problems that can affect conversion schemes. A sudden rise in interest rates, a sudden change in VAT rules, a new Fire Officer, the bankruptcy of a contractor, all these and many more can upset even the best planned scheme. Clearly it is not possible to take precautions against major upheavals, but it is necessary to be prepared for many minor changes.

- The first necessity is to know what is going on. A management committee meeting once a fortnight cannot adequately oversee a building project. The driving force should keep in constant touch with the work, partly out of sheer interest in the whole project, partly out of single minded determination to see it succeed.

- One of the essential considerations in judging whether a scheme is even worth considering initially is the condition of the building. Those who have to undertake the conversion of buildings in poor condition must plan for meeting unexpected problems, and must maintain adequate contingency funds.

- A typical response of an entrepreneur to uncertainty is to proceed in small steps – to try something and see if it works, and if it does to try some more. This leads to a phased approach, where the amount of construction work being undertaken at one time, and so the amount of capital at risk in case of disaster, is comparatively small.

- Phasing reduces the cash flow problems of a scheme as the timing of expenditures can be kept in step with the build up of revenues.

- Phasing also allows the driving force to be on the site – managing the completed phases – and so to keep in touch with later construction work.

- When changes or trade-offs have to be made it is important that the driving force knows about them, as they may affect the atmosphere or balance of the finished scheme more than anyone else can realise.

- The other consideration is cash flow. The effect of changes, including timing changes, on cash flow has to be watched (Case Study 10).

MANAGEMENT STAGE

It is during this stage that the scheme comes to fruition. It cannot be judged a success until its new uses are self sustaining. This entails finding suitable choose an architect who understands what you are trying to achieve and has a proven track record in managing contractors.

- A good quantity surveyor who also understands the entrepreneurial approach will be invaluable on large or complicated projects. The architect will usually have suitable contacts. A good quantity surveyor can give advice early on about any aspects of the scheme which will add greatly to the costs and how these might be modified.

- The cost of a project can be increased by 'cosmetic' work which is not fundamental to the scheme (e.g. external cleaning, landscaping). Unless these can be grant aided (Case Study 13), or are definitely needed to market the scheme, it may be wise to omit or delay them.

- It is possible to manage virtually without professionals (Case Study 7) and it is claimed this can lead to enormous cost savings, but most people prefer to use them and to avoid the risk of catastrophe. Furthermore when local authorities are closely involved, as they usually will be where schemes are grant aided, an architect is almost essential, as professionals wish to deal with other professionals.

- Many architects will undertake preliminary work on the understanding that it will only be paid for if the scheme goes ahead. Never be afraid to ask architects to work on this basis, if you are sure they are the right ones for the job.

- Use the professional team as consultants, and use them only when they will do a job better than you will.

> 'Professionals have their uses, but they do not normally have the time to think out your problem deeply enough. Do your own thinking. Use your own judgement. Keep control of all the things that are important.'

- A good scheme creates its own momentum, and those involved begin to feel that they are on a winning team. In some cases, for example, local authority officers almost became extra members of the team and contributed greatly to the scheme's success. (Case Studies 2, 4, 6, 10).

(7) Reliable contractor

The architect usually finds the contractor, but there are a great many possible variations ranging from 'do-it-yourself' (Case Study 7) and 'employing-your-friends' (Case Study 11) through to Design and Build (Case Studies 4, 8, 13) where the whole development team comes as a package. The characteristics of the different arrangements are discussed in, for example, *The Conversion Improvement and Extension of Buildings* by R. and S. Catt (19). Several points emerge from the case studies:

- A reliable contractor is vital. Experience and quality of on-site supervision are the main considerations. The lowest bid does not always give the best value. Make sure that you have checked out the contractor's previous work.

- It is perfectly possible to make the workforce feel part of the winning team, either because of the way it is organised or because of keen local interest (Case Studies 2, 7, 10, 11).

- Fixed price contracts, where the contractor undertakes to do the conversion for a given sum, regardless of their actual costs, can sometimes be negotiated (Case Study 4) or part of the scheme effectively subcontracted to a separate developer (Case Study 13) to reduce risks. On many conversion projects it may not be possible to obtain realistic fixed price bids. It is then necessary to understand how cost variations can occur under a standard contract (19) and to discuss in advance with the architect and quantity surveyor what sorts of changes you would be prepared to contemplate (and what you would not), if it became necessary to keep costs within limits.

- In spite of the obvious cost advantages, many schemes decided not to use an MSC workforce, except where training is a definite component of the project (Case Studies 2, 14). The reasons given were that it might slow the scheme down or just add another level of complication. However, there are now experienced MSC 'Managing Agents' who have established track records and good supervisors and who might be able to undertake conversion projects. They can be contacted through MSC regional offices. Many schemes, of course, are not eligible for direct MSC support, but it could be sensible to try to arrange for local environmental improvement work (which usually is eligible) to be co-ordinated with your scheme (Case Study 13).

CONSTRUCTION STAGE

This is the stage during which the building work is done. It may take a very short time (Case Studies 4, 10) or it may cover a period of years. If the first two stages have been properly carried out there will be less likelihood of problems occurring at this stage except those due to bad management or bad luck. The two key factors at this stage are:–

  (8)   Efficient Project Management
  (9)   Flexibility When Necessary.

(8) Efficient project management

Efficient project management means getting the job done on time and within budget, and depends mostly on the competence of the contractor and the ability of new users and keeping them. In some cases this may require no more than straight-forward marketing and management, in the case of housing or office use for example. But, in many cases, particularly where the scheme is innovative it is necessary to create the climate in which the users – the tenants or the visitors, perhaps – can succeed or enjoy themselves, and then continue to ensure that they do. In these circumstances, the final stage is more like starting and running a business than just managing or administering a building. Two key factors are:–

    (10)   Communication of excitement
    (11)   Management committed to success.

(10) Communication of excitement

For success, the excitement that has been behind the scheme through all its previous stages now has to be communicated to the potential users. The first requirement is that the scheme should indeed have turned out to be as exciting and viable as originally envisaged. It is for this reason that such stress has been placed on the long term commitment of the driving force. If that excitement and commitment are present there are many ways of communicating them.

- First it is necessary to be clear who it is important to communicate to. Work out who you need to attract. For example, is it just tenants, or customers for those tenants (Case Studies 6, 12, 13)?

- The overall message to communicate is usually

  'You too can join our success' or
  'This can be a special place for you'

  It must never be

  'Look how clever we were to do this scheme'

- As in any small business, it is essential to communicate what is special or distinctive about what you have to offer. You must differentiate your 'product' from the general commodity of 'space to let'.

- Local newspapers, local radio and even local television are always looking for items to cover. They can give excellent free publicity.

- Local networks always exist and can be effective channels of communication. Make sure that in the launching of the scheme you involve organisations such as the:–

  local enterprise agency
  local estate agents
  local tourist authority
  local voluntary associations.

- If it is necessary to attract the public, a scheme with a mixture of uses that complement each other has a head start (Case Studies 7, 12, 13).

- Special events may help to launch a scheme and to revive attention periodically, but their expense and the target audience must be kept in mind.

(11) Management committed to success

From the case studies it appears that there are two important but very different aspects of managing success

    External (continuing to foster the success of the users)
    Internal (the orderly management of the property).

- Where the users are basically tenants it is easy to combine these two through 'management by walking around' (Case Studies 1, 3, 6, 7, 11, 12, 14). This requires a scheme to be large enough to afford high calibre management, or to have some other device for ensuring supervision (Case Study 13).

- The driving force should continue to manage entrepeneurial projects at least until they are well established. It is possible to hand over the driving force role during the course of a project (Case Studies 5, 12).

- Occupancy is always an important determinant of profitability. Simple forms should be kept showing occupancy and yield at a glance (Case Studies 1, 12). Marketing should be geared to occupancy levels.

- Intensive use of a site or building can give rise to friction among users unless there is constant vigilance (Case Study 12).

- Where the users are people who visit the site, much greater emphasis has to be placed on continuing publicity and of finding ways to keep attracting people in.

- Attracting people in and orderly internal management are fundamentally different activities and need to be managed in different ways.

Further information on property management can be found in *Managing Workspaces* (1).

> **'Looking back, was it worth all the effort? Rationally, no of course it wasn't . . . but how else could you make such a wonderful place nowadays?'**

5   Summary of key factors

THREE ESSENTIAL REQUIREMENTS

- Adopt the appropriate development approach for the scheme.
- Make sure there is a committed driving force.
- Pick a building that is basically suitable for conversion.

INCUBATION STAGE

- Choose a balance of uses that maximises the use of space.
- Enlist the support of the local authority early on.
- Make sure that your scheme is viable and sustainable.
- Carry out a Feasibility Study if others need convincing.

NEGOTIATION STAGE

- Obtain the property on good terms.
- Look for finance from all available sources.
- Use grants to make innovative schemes work.
- Choose a sound professional team.
- Make sure that a reliable contractor is chosen.
- Abandon the scheme if the above conditions are not met.

CONSTRUCTION STAGE

- Ensure that the building works are closely overseen.
- Carry out the project in phases where possible.
- Watch the cash flow projections regularly.

MANAGEMENT STAGE

- Promote the scheme tirelessly.
- Manage the building in an orderly way.
- Continue to foster the success of the users.

Case Study 1: The Argent Centre, Birmingham; a conversion of a listed factory to small industrial, commercial and office units

Case Study 2: Curzon Street Station, Birmingham; a Grade 1 listed station providing training workshops and voluntary organisation offices

Case Study 3: Dean Clough, Halifax; a huge textile mill being re-used as an industrial estate for small firms, with various support services

Case Study 4: Imperial Studies, Hammersmith; a bus depot converted for small workshops, offices and studio units for high technology firms

Case Study 5: Mantra House, Keighley; a 1930's engineering works used as small units, with office support services

Case Study 6: The Briggait, Glasgow; a listed fish market now re-used as a speciality shopping centre with food hall

Case Study 7: Waterfront Hotel, Hull; a 19th century listed warehouse now re-used as hotel, restaurant and night club

surveyors who advised them still concluded that re-use was unsatisfactory compared with redevelopment. This was largely because of the institutional approach to development, when what was needed was a more entrepreneurial approach. This finding came out clearly in research which URBED undertook in 1979 for the Hackney/Islington Partnership which showed how entrepreneurs were making a success of bringing buildings back into use by phasing the development and keeping their costs to the minimum, even though a major firm of estate agents had concluded in almost every case that redevelopment was unviable (4).

Lessons from the USA

Several of the ideas that have been gaining ground in Britain have their roots in the USA. In America the 'recycling' of old industrial buildings is a well established way of creating industrial space for new industry and other uses. A well known example is Lowell, Massachusetts, a mill town which has been brought back to life largely by new private users taking advantage of a wide range of public sector financial incentives. Even major American companies are happy to use refurbished mills as headquarters or production plants, whereas in Britain few large companies would do so.

Another idea to come from the USA is the packaging of the finance from different sources and using public finance to 'lever' private investment. In Britain, Urban Development Grant is based on this principle, although in the USA tax incentives are far more important. Closely allied to leverage is the idea of public/private joint ventures or partnerships, which has been taken up in Britain through the establishment of Development Trusts (5).

A third American idea, which has still to be widely copied in Britain, is the idea of converting buildings into places where people can buy unusual products or food – what the developer of Baltimore's Waterfront and Boston's Quincy Market calls 'Festival Marketplaces'. Covent Garden in London was Britain's first response.

A fourth idea is that of having mixed uses in the same building, especially workspace and residential accommodation. Orthodox planning in Britain has been against this, but many old buildings can be adapted quite naturally to a range of uses.

Basic Concepts and Trends

Thus although the re-use movement has only made serious progress in Britain during the past 20 years, there have already been a number of clear trends in the uses to which converted buildings have been put, as the case studies in the second part of this report illustrate. Initially interest was confined to museums and galleries (Case Study 13). Then, as explained

above, it shifted to the conversion of buildings into workspace for small firms. In recent years, a wide range of types of workspace have emerged. These include community workshops where people can learn a skill, innovation centres with links to colleges, enterprise centres or workshops with supporting services provided, and various kinds of business centres, which are essentially serviced office suites or miniature industrial estates (Case Studies 1, 3, 4, 5, 11, 12).

More recently a number of other uses have begun to emerge. For example, in Manchester a multi-storey 19th Century warehouse has been converted into television studios. Warehouses and mills can also make fine housing. The first examples, such as Oliver's Wharf in London, were aimed at well-off people who did not require mortgages. However, in the past few years, there have been examples in places such as Hull, Lancaster and Manchester (Case Study 9), and schemes for rented flats in Huddersfield and Ipswich (Case Study 10). This trend has developed not only because of a demand for distinctive places to live, but also to provide housing in city centres for young people and business people and because building societies are now more willing to make mortgages available on converted properties.

Recreational uses are also growing in importance. As well as speciality shopping centres such as Covent Garden in London and The Briggait in Glasgow (Case Study 6), there are also galleries and sports centres, which require large areas of cheap, flexible space (Case Study 14). As yet there are only a few examples of conversions into hotels and hostels (Case Study 7), but undoubtedly these too will increase as people come to appreciate the character that can be created in old buildings. Other new uses are emerging, such as community centres and recording studios, and in the future there will undoubtedly be mixed work and living schemes, whose beginnings can already be seen in London's docklands.

In fact it has now been shown that in the right circumstances old industrial and commercial buildings can be converted to virtually every imaginable type of use, often with considerable side benefits as well. However, there is also an underlying trend of realism, for only a fraction of the empty buildings that scar our landscape can hope to be brought back into suitable use in the forseeable future. More care is therefore being given to seeing that efforts are focussed on schemes that are likely to succeed or where there are special factors which justify a public subsidy.

Just as there has been a recent widening of the types of buildings converted and in the uses to which they are being put, so there has been a parallel expansion of the types of bodies undertaking conversion schemes. While some commercial development firms are involved, more and more local authorities, voluntary groups and even private individuals are also taking on conversion schemes, often with financial support from the Urban Programme. And as the case studies show the local authority nearly always has an important part to play.

Trends in the local authority's role

Local authorities are now deeply involved in economic as well as physical development. The re-use of redundant buildings is of vital interest to them. Many local authorities therefore have undertaken their own conversion schemes, but many are now looking at ways of encouraging such schemes without becoming directly involved in them themselves. Three trends can be observed.

First there is the preparation of strategies, and this is most noticeable in areas where there are large concentrations of empty buildings. The first step is usually to take stock of the problems and the realistic opportunities, then to set about mobilising public funding, from all available sources, and private enthusiasm. A strategy is an important device in this process. For example, Urban Programme funding might be used in combination with money from other sources, such as English Heritage (for the structure), the Tourist Boards (for visitor facilities), the MSC (for environmental improvements) and in many cases the EEC (for matching conversion costs). In all these cases the funding sources will want to know if the proposed individual projects are part of a concerted strategy. Furthermore the preparation of such a strategy by the local authority, in consultation with building owners and the local community, can help not only to co-ordinate different departments but also to encourage the property owners to contribute through their own actions, which they are much more likely to do when they can see them as part of a larger collaborative effort. This has proved successful, for example, in Industrial Improvement Areas, but is also being used on a wider scale.

Secondly, where funds have to be packaged from different sources there is a growing use of trusts to promote and organise schemes (Case Studies 6, 8, 14). In many cases local authorities are encouraging the formation of such trusts and channelling their own contributions through them.

Finally where exciting but unconventional schemes are proposed for difficult buildings, the local authority's flexibility can sometimes make all the difference between failure and success. Many local authorities are taking a more positive and enabling attitude towards development. The case studies show many examples of this, and the mixed workspace and residential schemes that are starting to be approved are further evidence of this greater flexibility.

All these trends have led to some interesting and successful schemes as these case studies show, and one way of maintaining the momentum is to enable newcomers, who often have no experience of property development whatsoever, to learn the lessons of those who have gone before.

3 Understanding the conversion process

Property development

Converting an old building to a new use is basically a property development. Yet many who undertake conversions, and especially those doing so with funding under the Urban Programme, have little or no direct experience of property development. Indeed they may even despise 'developers' and 'property development', associating them with repetitive, uninspiring buildings and quick profits! This chapter, therefore, briefly describes the development process and provides a framework within which good practices can be discussed.

Property development, the masterminding of a building-based scheme right through from inception to completion, is a complicated process involving many different tasks. It is described in detail by Cadmam and Austin-Crowe (6), for example. It requires knowledge, judgement, skill and persistence, and it might therefore be assumed that nobody could be successful at it who has not had long professional training, but in practice this is not the case at all. Rather it seems that there are certain basic elements of a scheme which form the framework and which need to be right, but within that framework it is possible for even an inexperienced developer to complete projects successfully by bringing in professional help when appropriate. We shall therefore describe the conversion process in terms of:

- Three Essential Requirements
    Appropriate Development Approach
    Driving Force
    Suitable Building

- Four Stages of a Project
    Incubation Stage
    Negotiation Stage
    Construction Stage
    Management Stage

It is hoped that this framework will be useful to those who are trying to encourage new schemes as well as to those who are considering undertaking one themselves. In this chapter the three essential requirements are discussed first, with particular reference to conversion schemes, but it has long been recognised that even in conventional property development there are a few basic factors which are much more important than others. If they are not right from the outset it is unlikely that the scheme will succeed. As estate agents often say:

'There are only three things that matter in property: location, location, location.'

Appropriate development approach

Although conversion schemes are property developments it must be clearly understood that there are at least two fundamentally different approaches to development (4, 7), the conventional (or 'institutional') approach and the entrepreneurial approach. In most cases conversion schemes will be forced to adopt an entrepreneurial approach, and while many of the detailed steps will be similar in both cases (indeed there is much that the entrepreneur can learn from the sheer professionalism of the conventional approach), there are fundamental differences which must be appreciated if the entire scheme is not to start off on the wrong footing.

Conventional approach

The essence of the conventional approach is that it is entirely geared to the production of a building which will be bought as an investment by a financial institution. An important requirement, from the point of view of the institution, is that its investments must be readily saleable should the need arise. It will therefore only invest in properties which meet strict criteria regarding such things as their location, their ability to be used by a broad category of users, and even their methods of construction. In other words, institutions want to invest in marketable commodities, and the task of the conventional developer is to produce the right commodity in the right place as quickly and efficiently as possible. The main skills required are in:

- spotting market trends

- negotiating (particularly with regard to acquisition of sites, planning permission and financing arrangements)

- understanding all the rules

- co-ordinating for speed.

The main tasks involved in the conventional development process are shown in Table 2. The conventional developer tends to put a great deal of effort into assembling resources, working out all the details of the scheme, and tying down all the relationships (including the terms under which a particular institution will buy the completed building) in advance, so that once the development begins it can go ahead as quickly and smoothly as possible.

This conventional approach usually applies to new building. However there are some cases where it is appropriate for conversion schemes (Case Studies 4, 9).

Table 2: Tasks in the conventional development process

1 Perception and Estimation of Demand for New Commercial Buildings.

2 Identification of Sites.

3 Acquisition of Site.

4 Design of Scheme.

5 Arrangement of Finance.

6 Management of Construction.

7 Letting of Completed Building.

8 Disposal of Property as Investment.

(Based on *Commercial Property Development* (*The Pilcher Report*) pp 49-50, HMSO, London, 1975).

Entrepreneurial approach

A different approach is required where there is little or no likelihood of an institution buying the completed scheme, or if the developer has no intention of selling it. In that case the whole focus of the development must be on ensuring the success of whatever end-use is planned for the building. Thus the building becomes only a means to an end, and the real task of the developer is to develop the end-use of the building and make it a success. It involves a very different type of commitment than under the conventional approach, because it is more like starting and running a business rather than just developing a building. For this reason we call it the entrepreneurial approach,

and, judging from the case studies, the main skills required are in:

- perceiving viable end-uses

- creating enthusiasm and excitement

- reacting to opportunities and being flexible

- maintaining momentum over a long period.

The entrepreneurial developer needs a clear vision of what is to be achieved, but is prepared to be flexible over how it is achieved. If possible, initial investment will be kept low, and development will be phased over time so as to keep it in step with demand and maintain an adequate return on investment. All the time the developer will be looking for new ways of increasing demand, just as any entrepreneur would, and may seek to encourage several different types of use simultaneously if that helps to generate more activity and better use of the site. The entrepreneurial approach, therefore, may often lead to mixed use schemes, and if so skill in balancing mixed uses is required.

As the previous chapter explained there are few financial institutions that are prepared to invest in converted industrial property. Thus in the great majority of cases those undertaking conversion schemes must take the entrepreneurial approach, for if they cannot sell their completed schemes then they must take responsibility for operating them. Furthermore most of the industrial or commercial buildings that are candidates for conversion will be:

- redundant, with no obvious use as they presently stand

- in poor locations, where business once flourished but no longer does, or alternatively

- listed buildings in better locations.

These are 'problem' buildings which entrepreneurs may turn into opportunities. The case studies describe how this has been done by different people and organisations in differing circumstances. In most cases a basically entrepreneurial approach was taken, which meant that involvement in the commitment to the end-use of the building was as important, if not more important, than the actual conversion itself.

Professional vs. amateur approach

Although there are fundamental differences between the conventional and entrepreneurial approaches to development, they both have one major factor in common. They are both dealing with a complicated process where there is plenty of scope for errors. Both require constant attention to detail in a thoroughly professional manner. Just because the normal approach to conversion schemes is called 'entrepreneurial' this should in no way be thought to imply amateurism or a lack of single-minded determination. If anything, conversion requires more professionalism not less.

> Question: 'What is the easiest way of making a small fortune out a conversion scheme?'
>
> Answer: 'Start with a large fortune.'

Driving force

The second essential requirement for successful property development is a driving force by which we mean an individual or team that 'carries the vision' of a scheme right through to its successful conclusion and is more than either a promoter or a project manager. Complicated schemes do not happen by themselves. They happen because somebody makes them happen. In virtually all the case studies it is possible to identify a driving force, and it is usually an individual or an individual leading a team. Driving forces can be found even in local authority schemes (Case Studies 2, 13). A really cohesive group can act as driving force (Case Study 11), but not all voluntary groups that start out cohesively remain that way (8).

The driving force is not just a figurehead, but is singlemindedly committed to the overall success of the scheme, and would appear to be just as important in conventional development (Case Studies 4, 9) as when an entrepreneurial approach is adopted. But the commitment required in the entrepreneurial case may be even greater because it means staying on until the end-use achieves success. The driving force, therefore, needs to 'carry the vision' of the end-use right through the entire project.

Different skills and personal characteristics are required in the different stages of a conversion scheme. Occasionally one individual may be able to cover the full range (Case Studies 7, 14) but often ways have to be found to:

- bring others into a team either temporarily or permanently (Case Studies 1, 2, 3, 4, 9, 10, 11), or

- divide the whole scheme into parallel projects (Case Studies 8, 13), or

- pass the role of driving force sequentially from one person to another (Case Studies 5, 8, 12).

> **'It's your scheme. You have got to make it happen. Nobody else can do that for you'.**

A person who sets up a marvellous scheme but fails to see that it is taken right through to a sustainable end-use is not an adequate driving force. Care must therefore be taken when a scheme is being considered to ensure that there is a means of providing a driving force which runs right through the project and is committed to the end-use. Also it must be ensured that the driving force does have the ability and the authority to control the direction of the scheme otherwise it can fall between two stools.

Most of the driving forces described in the case studies are perfectly ordinary people. The main qualities required would seem to be a little vision, a little enthusiasm and a great deal of determination. Anyone can be a driving force.

> **'Genius is one per cent inspiration and ninety-nine per cent perspiration'.**

Suitable building

Just as location is a crucial factor in conventional property development, so in conversion schemes it is vital to start with a suitable building. Of course there are special situations which justify rescuing particular buildings however unsuitable they may be, and the case studies show that with the help of government subsidies viable schemes can sometimes be devised even in difficult situations (Case Studies 2, 6). But not every old building is really special and it would be a waste of time and effort to try to devise schemes for buildings which do not stand a chance. A noticeable factor in the case studies was that quite often the driving force 'knew' that the building was right on the very first visit. It is useful to be able to judge right at the outset whether a building is likely to be capable of re-use, and for what.

The main factors which need to be considered are

- location

- configuration

- condition.

There are other basic factors such as the attitudes of the owner of the building and the local authority, but these vary from case to case and may be subjects for negotiation. These three are basic characteristics of the building.

Location
Buildings which are not close to a source of activity are difficult to re-use unless there is some very good reason to attract the users (Case Study 6). However, many redundant buildings are quite well located and within easy reach of centres of population (most Case Studies).

Furthermore, location refers not just to the part of the country or type of neighbourhood in which a building stands, but also to the attractiveness of an area to different types of use. A factor which would rule out one use could be an advantage for another, and the most successful schemes are those that respond to what potential customers will be looking for. For example, an old waterside warehouse will often be in the centre of a town and surrounded by narrow streets. This location is probably unsuitable for industry, but may be quite acceptable as a place to live where the view over water will be appreciated, or as a place of entertainment (Case Study 7).

It does not usually take sophisticated market research to know whether a building is in a good location, but schemes involving out-of-the-way buildings or those in disagreeable surroundings need to be scrutinised very carefully.

Configuration

The shape and size of the building are very important. Most uses will want natural light, and the distance from windows may well determine how much of a building can be re-used. Basically, the cheaper and simpler a building, the more difficult it will be to provide natural lighting and means of fire escape without expensive modifications. Often the most easily re-used buildings are those that form complexes, where a phased approach can start in the easiest parts. (Case Studies 3, 7, 12). Sometimes a building with a difficult shape can be made useable by cutting a lightwell in it (Case Study 10). Alternatively some sites can be greatly improved by selective demolition (Case Studies 1, 2, 3, 5).

Overall the two main considerations are the depth of the building and the ceiling heights. These can be assessed very quickly, without even going inside the building.

Condition

Probably the most important variable is the condition of the building. Previous URBED studies have shown that it is the costs of renovation, as opposed to conversion, that vary most between different projects (4, 9). The longer a building is left empty, the greater and more expensive will be the work required. At first the problem tends to be vandalism, then the theft of lead from the roof, causing water to penetrate. In time rot sets in. Fires, too, may damage the roof, accelerating the process of decay. A building may stand empty for several years without problems and then quickly become worthless. The state of the services inside the building is usually not important, as they will generally have to be replaced anyway, but the presence of adequate sewers can make a major difference to the viability of a scheme.

From the case studies it can be seen that the buildings chosen were usually structurally sound. This was not always so (Case Studies 2, 6, 11) but in such cases it was hard to attract private finance and in one instance required a 'do-it-yourself' approach to be taken (Case Study 7). Again it is not too difficult to tell at the outset if a building is in a basically sound condition, and therefore worth persevering with.

However, a proper survey would certainly need to be done later when calculating the costs of a scheme.

Role of Urban Programme funding

The Urban Programme is one of the main channels through which central government provides extra money to help combat special problems in the major towns and cities in England (see Appendix D). One such problem is the blight caused by empty industrial buildings which have outlived their original purpose. Furthermore, since schemes by local authorities, voluntary organisations, and in some circumstances private developers, can receive Urban Programme funding, and since the Programme's emphasis is increasingly on capital investment projects, many industrial building conversion schemes do receive support in this way. Understanding Urban Programme funding is therefore very relevant to understanding the conversion process.

There are two ways in which the support can be given:

- Urban Programme (UP): A capital grant (and occasionally a revenue grant as well) to enable local authorities or voluntary assocations to undertake approved schemes, often of an innovative nature. As there is almost never any intention or likelihood of selling such schemes to an investor an entrepreneurial approach is usually required (Case Studies 5, 11, 13, 14). Although UP schemes can be phased over several years there is a tendency for complete schemes to be undertaken at one time. This contrasts with the truly entrepreneurial approach taken when little or no public money is involved (Case Studies 3, 7, 12).

- Urban Development Grant (UDG): a capital grant or loan intended to provide just enough subsidy to a developer to enable an approved scheme to go ahead in locations where it would not normally be able to. Here the strategy is to encourage a more conventional development approach (Case Study 4, 9). In some other cases UDG (or its Scottish equivalent, LEG-UP) has been used to support the entrepreneurial approach in a way that is very similar to ordinary Urban Programme funding (Case Studies 1, 6).

More information about Urban Programme funding can be found in, for example, *Raising Money From Government*, published by the Directory of Social Change (10).

Local authority schemes

Local authorities undertake many conversion schemes and since they are able to raise their own money on a large scale it might be imagined that they could follow any development approach they chose. In practice, however, local authorities' finances are under considerable strain. In particular they cannot necessarily afford to set up schemes which they will have to go on subsidising indefinitely into the future. Thus they also are looking very closely at the end-uses of their development schemes and are being forced to take more of an entrepreneurial approach.

4   A guide to good practices

Stages in the conversion process

Once the three essential requirements of the conversion process are understood, consideration can be given as to how to set about planning and carrying out a conversion process step by step. Following an entrepreneurial approach there are four main sets of activities to get right, and these may conveniently be referred to as the Four Stages of the project

- Planning a viable scheme   (INCUBATION STAGE)

- Obtaining the resources   (NEGOTIATION STAGE)

- Carrying out the conversion   (CONSTRUCTION STAGE)

- Making the end-use a success (MANAGEMENT STAGE)

At each stage many different inputs and tasks may be required. Detailed lists are provided in, for example, Eley and Worthington's *Industrial Rehabilitation* (11) or Green and Foley's *Redundant Space - a Productive Asset* (12). However it is the achievements at each stage, rather than the inputs, which are important, and the case studies indicate that there are comparatively few achievements which are truly important. They are shown in Table 3 and it is on these key factors for success that the discussion of good practices is focussed.

The case studies show that the driving force plays a key role throughout the project, but that the level of direct involvement tends to vary from stage to stage. The Incubation Stage is basically the responsibility of the driving force alone, usually drawing in an architect and the local authority. During the Negotiation Stage the driving force assembles the people and resources required and works closely with the architect.

The Construction Stage is usually left principally to the architect and other professionals and the contractor. There are, however, examples of much greater involvement by the driving force (Case Studies 7, 10, 14). Where an entrepreneurial approach is taken the driving force becomes crucially involved again at the Management Stage, at least until the scheme is

well established and successful. In about half the case studies the same person who initiated the scheme ended up managing it. Thus those who start out on entrepreneurial conversion schemes must be prepared for a long haul. They must be prepared to take overall responsibility, but provided they can afford it they can use professionals to carry out most of the tasks related to the construction work.

Good practices

In the following sections good practices are described for each stage and in the case studies most of the good practices can be seen in action. However, there are often several different ways of achieving the same end and it is seldom possible to state categorically that one practice is superior to all others. Futhermore, there is scarcely any area in which the case studies do not provide at least one example of a scheme which totally ignored what is here described as good practice and yet succeeded very well.

Good practices are merely guidelines to help those who lack experience or confidence. For this reason we have tried to concentrate on the key issues at each stage and we have tried to explain the intention behind the good practice as well as the techniques that might be applied.

INCUBATION STAGE

This is the stage during which a conversion scheme is thought through, right through to the end-uses. The basic idea may have been in someone's mind for a long time, but at some point the new use and the building must be brought together and a viable scheme developed for achieving and maintaining it. The exact steps will depend on how the project originated, but this usually occurs through:

- an individual (or group) wishing to promote a new activity which requires a building, or

Case Study 8: Watershed, Bristol; 19th Century dockside warehouse re-used as a media centre, radio station and shopping units

Case Study 9: Granby House, Manchester; a listed Edwardian warehouse converted by a housing association for first time buyers

Case Study 10: Pipers Court, Ipswich; a Victorian clothing factory re-used to provide flats for rental and sale

Case Study 11: Bradbury Street, Hackney; a derelict row of buildings rehabilitated by a co-operative development agency for local shops and offices

studies however show that the buildings were attractive because they were in good structural condition.

- Projects which start from a use in search of a building are likely to be easier to make successful than those that start from the idea of saving a building. But there are good examples of the latter succeeding too (Case Studies 2, 10, 13, 14).

The reason for a building becoming redundant in its old form was that it did not attract sufficient sustainable use. The trick of making the building a success again, therefore, is to find new uses for all its spaces.

- Virtually all the schemes in the case studies contain mixed uses of one form or another. This often enabled users to benefit from each other either directly or indirectly, or from the additional customer-pulling power of other uses. It also enabled full use to be made of different types of space.

- Food and drink attract customers. In half the case studies there was alcohol for sale.

- Avoid obvious bad neighbour industries (Case Studies 3, 4, 12), but remember also that densely used sites need constant management attention to avoid disputes (Case Studies 3, 12) and that craft workers usually do not like having their work interrupted by streams of visitors (Case Studies 6, 12, 13).

- Visit other conversion schemes and see what works and what does not. This is one of the best methods of learning.

- Read about what has been done further afield. There is a growing bibliography (Appendix A).

Table 4: Example of windscreen survey worksheet						
VACANT BUILDING SURVEY						
ADDRESS						
GROSS FLOOR AREA						
PRESENT USE					% of VACANCY	
PREVIOUS USE						
TENURE						
	++	+	o	−	− −	
Off Street Parking & Delivery		√				On street Parking Narrow
60% Site Coverage		√				100% Site Coverage
Good Site Access	√					No Site Access
5 min. Tube and Bus		√				10 min. Bus
Goods lift/Wide Staircase				√		No Lifts/Narrow Staircase
Single Storied			√			4 or more Stories
ACCESS	√					
Four way Aspect		√				Single Aspect
10 – 15 m. Deep	√					20 m. or More Deep
Simple Shape			√			Complex Shape
3.00 m. FL/FL (Upper Floor)	√					3.60 m. + FL/FL
CONFIGURATION	√					
Frame				√		Load Bearing Walls
Brick, Concrete Plasterboard		√				Timber, Cast Iron, Steel
STRUCTURE						
CONDITION Good			√			Bad
PROPOSED OUTCOME						

Based on URBED, *Recycling Industrial Buildings* (Capital Planning Information, 1981)

Case Study 12: Camden Lock, Camden; Victorian stables and warehouses re-used as craft workshops, market, dance hall and cultural centre, using private finance

Case Study 13: Canal Museum, Nottingham; an old canal warehouse and stables converted to house a museum, workshop units, pub and restaurant

Case Study 14: Pallion Residents Enterprises, Sunderland; the conversion by local residents of a vacant post-war clothing factory into sports facilities and units for small firms

- If the initiators of a scheme are not entirely convinced of its success they should prepare as honest a feasibility study as they can, taking into account the three essential requirements discussed in Chapter 3 and all the key factors for success listed in Table 3. Then decide whether or not to proceed. Often the scheme can be refined and improved at this stage, for example by changing the balance of uses, by phasing the work differently or by plugging a loophole, and this can help increase confidence at what is often a very worrying stage. It costs nothing to alter a scheme at this stage. Making changes later can be very expensive, and there is nothing more costly than proceeding with a scheme that basically will not work.

- All feasibility studies apart from your own personal assessment should be regarded as selling documents, and those evaluating them should not only probe the assumptions on which they are based but also check how likely it is that the key achievements will be met.

- Pay particular attention to the timing of cash outflows and inflows. The golden rule of business is: DO NOT RUN OUT OF CASH.

- When estimating future revenues, be realistic about the length of time it will take for the building to fill up. Although many of the case studies show that high occupancy was rapidly achieved, it would be unwise to assume this or that occupancy will ever reach 100%.

- Where substantial conversion costs are foreseen, get an experienced builder or a professional quantity surveyor to estimate the costs. An architect may be persuaded to postpone any fees until the project goes ahead, but it is more difficult to get surveyors or quantity surveyors to do anything without payment.

- Pay particular attention to the requirement and costs of Fire Regulations. Fire safety standards have increased greatly since most old buildings were built, and the cost of bringing them up to modern standards may be prohibitive.

- The main factors to pay attention to are the provision of fire escape routes (including inside the building, not just outside), ensuring that the structural elements of the building are adequately fire resistant, and ensuring adequate fire resistance between different units and different uses.

- Fire Officers sometimes have different opinions about the exact precautions required, such as, for example, whether cast iron columns can be retained without being encased. If there is some requirement which has a critical effect on the cost or visual impact of your scheme, telephone other schemes to try to find a precedent for your solution and negotiate directly with the Fire Officer.

- When estimating building costs pay particular attention to the way in which the work will be organised. Professionals, a project manager, listed building status, etc. all add to costs, as do marketing costs, financing costs (interest payment during construction and letting) and contingency which must be allowed for realistically.

- Identify and involve the key people as early as possible, particularly any who may eventually take over the role of driving force.

The case studies show how a range of viable schemes were put together under the direction of a driving force. Formal feasibility studies were usually only prepared when required for attracting external funds, particularly government grants.

NEGOTIATION STAGE

This is the stage during which the external resources necessary to carry out the conversion scheme are secured. Negotiations can be carried out simultaneously on several fronts, but the final point of no return is the acquisition of the building.

During this stage it may be necessary to modify the scheme in order to accommodate the requirements of those providing the resources. If so the effect on the scheme, and in particular its long term viability, must be carefully considered. The driving force, who carries the vision of the scheme, must agree any trade-offs that are made. The commitment to the success and viability of the end-use must remain.

Although there will be periods of frantic activity, this stage like its predecessor can take a very long time. This is especially true if grants are required, but buying a building and raising private sector finance can also take an extraordinarily long time (Case Studies 1, 6). Staying alive and maintaining enthusiasm during this stage can be a very real problem. That is why it is sensible to arrange a preliminary income generating activity or to plan the project in stages with emphasis on early income generation (Case Studies 1, 3, 7, 12). Revenue grants to help set up capital schemes are unfortunately not easy to obtain.

The key factors for success for this stage are:

(4) Good Property Terms
(5) Flexible Financial Package
(6) Sound Professional Team
(7) Reliable Contractor

(4) Good property terms
Obtaining the right building on the right terms is obviously fundamental.

- The most crucial point is for the organisations which are going to invest money and effort into the property to have the necessary legal rights to it, and any important surrounding land, and on the right terms. If a freehold is required, for example to provide security for a bank mortgage, insist on a freehold. If the local authority will buy the building or take a head lease, insist on a suitable lease from them. Always use a lawyer to check the legal and contractual arrangements, but not necessarily to carry out all the preliminary negotiations.

- Price is also important, particularly if there is substantial private investment. Most redundant buildings are worth little more than their demolition value and can probably be bought cheaply. Some even have a negative value (Case Study 2). Owners often believe that their properties are more valuable than they really are ('Hope Value') and it may not be possible to negotiate an acceptable price. These principles apply:-

  Never pay more than other equivalent buildings are going for. Check out other property prices.

  Never pay more for the building than the amount that will just allow the scheme to be viable (Case Study 1).

  The longer the building remains unsold the more inclined the owner will be to drop the price. Negotiate persistently.

- If you are taking a lease make sure that you understand the cost implications of any conditions imposed by the lease. Tell your lawyer what you think the implications are and let him correct you if necessary. This helps to avoid misunderstandings.

- If you are taking a lease you may be able to link the rent you pay to the success of your operation (up to a stated limit) (Case Studies 6, 8) or even to obtain an initial rent free period (Case Study 6).

- So long as little additional investment is required, taking a short lease initially may be acceptable. This allows the project a chance to establish its viability, and if it does it will then be in a position to pay the best price for a longer lease or even a freehold (Case Study 12).

- If the right terms and price cannot be obtained, do not go ahead with the scheme. Like politics, entrepreneurship is the art of the possible.

(5) Flexible Financial Package

There are many potential sources of finance, but with the exception of the public sector most are cautious about conversion schemes. The case studies provide examples of a range of funding sources as shown in Table 5.

Table 5:   Sources of funds for case study schemes

Public sector

–Urban Programme (UP)	Case Studies 2, 4, 5, 11, 13, 14
–Urban Development Grant (UDG)	Case Studies 1, 6, 9
–Manpower Services Commission	Case Studies 2, 13, 14
–Historic Buildings Commission	Case Studies 6, 7, 8
–Improvement Grant (Housing)	Case Study 10
–EEC (ERDF)	Case Study 14
–Quango (BFI, ETB, Sports Cncl.)	Case Studies 7, 8, 14
–Local Authority	Case Studies 2, 5, 6, 11, 14
	(Plus Contribution through Urban Programme)

Private sector

–Bank Loan	Case Studies 1, 4, 8, 10,12
–Building Society	Case Studies 9, 10
–Brewery Loan	Case Studies 7, 14
–Property Fund	Case Study 4
–Insurance Company	Case Studies 6, 8
–Own Resources/Equity	Case Studies 3, 4, 7, 8, 10, 12, 13

Other sources

–Housing Association	Case Studies 9, 10
–Commercial Sponsorship	Case Studies 8, 14
–Fund Raising/Charities	Case Study 6

Note: It is also possible to obtain financial support for small schemes in certain rural areas from CoSIRA.

Further information on sources of finance can be found in some of the books listed in Appendix A (10, 12, 13, 14, 15, 16).

The important points are to raise enough money for the scheme and to try to obtain a certain amount of flexibility to allow the scheme to react to unexpected problems or opportunities. Grants have the special attraction that they do not have to be repaid (although there can sometimes be claw-back out of excessive profits), but they tend to have rigid requirements which reduce flexibility.

- Always approach the local authority during the Incubation Stage and discuss the possibility of getting a grant. Private developers are eligible for some grants, including UDG.

- When applying for grants or any form of finance build in enough money to the costs to enable the scheme to be managed right through until it is self-sustaining. Make sure that you have made proper allowance for the cost of marketing, managing and financing the scheme and for realistic occupancy levels.

- Be prepared to package finance from different sources. It is rare to find some single source which will provide all the funding. Approach many sources.

- Different funding bodies have different requirements. It may therefore be possible to build a logical sequence of funding (Case Studies 4, 6, 10, 14).

- Because different funding bodies have different requirements different applications for support will have to be prepared and submitted at different times. Do check the precise requirements, and break the scheme down clearly into elements that the different bodies can back.

- Urban Programme is an important potential source of funding for conversion schemes, but some local authorities require applications to be made in May for funds which cannot start until the following April. Sometimes some local authorities are able to obtain underspent funds at short notice late in the financial year. Discuss your ideas with the local authority at a very early stage.

- Voluntary groups should always have somebody on their management or advisory committee who is familiar with appropriate sources of finance. This not only enables the right approaches to be made to the different sources, but helps to build credibility. In the end though it is the commitment and vision of the driving force and the basic viability of the scheme which will attract financial support.

- If flexible funding, such as equity or personal money, cannot be raised, then the conversion work should be carried out in a flexible way, either by phasing (Case Studies 1, 3, 7, 11, 12) or by cutting back on some aspects of the work to allow unexpected costs to be covered (Case Studies 1, 7) or possibly by using an MSC workforce for a flexible period of time (Case Studies 2, 14).

'You never really know what you are going to find next with an old building, but if you really keep your eyes open you can see ways of saving money just as much as spending it'

- Prepare simple cash flow projections, and agree them with the principal providers of funds and with whoever is responsible for controlling the costs of conversion. Update them frequently.

(6) Sound professional team

Every conversion scheme will need an architect, and the architect can make an outstanding contribution to the scheme (Case Studies 4, 6, 10, 13). The quantity surveyor, who predicts and controls costs, also plays a crucial role in schemes that are at all complicated. There may be a professional Project Manager to oversee the building works (Case Studies 5, 6, 9, 10, 14), and other professional experts. A good team is obviously a great advantage. There are two points to consider:-

Finding appropriate professionals
Using them effectively.

- Choosing the right architect is the key, for an architect can usually find other professionals who will work with him or her. The architect will usually be prepared to manage the building contract as well as designing the scheme, but there are many other possibilities (11, 17).

- Experienced developers already know architects and how to use them. Local authorities usually use their own internal departments. Inexperienced developers should look for an architect who is not only competent, but whose work they like and who in turn is excited and interested by the scheme. The best approach is to look at other schemes which seem successful and find out about their architects from the people who undertook them (Case Study 1). As there are now many architects who have undertaken schemes or worked with community groups, lists are beginning to become available (18). The Royal Institute of British Architects (RIBA), the architects' official body, can also provide names (Case Study 11).

- The role of the architect is to take the driving force's vision and turn it into building plans. This requires a lot of work and thought by the driving force. The architect is not the developer (except where the developer happens to be an architect). The architect is the leader of the professional team, the driving force must manage the architect.

'An architect is only as good as their client'

- Sometimes it is the excellence of the architect's work that makes a scheme exciting (Case Studies 4, 10, 13), but more often it is the vision and enthusiasm of the driving force for the scheme. Therefore try to

17

Case studies

1   Argent Centre, Birmingham

2   Curzon Street Station, Birmingham

3   Dean Clough, Halifax

4   Imperial Studios, London

5   Mantra House, Bradford

6   The Briggait, Glasgow

7   Waterfront Hotel, Hull

8   Watershed, Bristol

9   Granby House, Manchester

10 Pipers Court, Ipswich

11 Bradbury Street, London

12 Camden Lock, London

13 Canal Museum, Nottingham

14 Pallion, Sunderland

Case studies

Each case study describes the conversion and re-use of an old industrial or commercial building, explains how the scheme was devised and organised, and highlights points of special interest in the four stages of the project:

- Incubation Stage   (Planning a viable scheme)

- Negotiation Stage   (Obtaining the resources)

- Construction Stage   (Carrying out the conversion)

- Management Stage   (Making the end-use a success)

Standard information is also included for quick reference:

- Good Practices Highlighted

- The Key Facts

- A Project Summary

- Notes (if applicable) and Project References

Each case study is self-contained and may be read by itself. In some instances a Note to one case study may also be relevant to another. For convenience, the Notes for all the case studies have been included in Appendix C.

The case studies have been grouped according to their major new use:

- Workspaces (Case studies 1 to 5)

- Leisure and retail (Case Studies 6 to 8)

- Housing (Case Studies 9 and 10)

- Mixed use (Case Studies 11 to 14)

A colour photograph of each case study is bound between Chapter 5 and the case studies.

1   Argent Centre

Frederick St., Birmingham

Grade II* Listed factory, now re-used as small industrial, commercial and office units. Developed by a non-profit Industrial Association using public and private finance.

GOOD PRACTICES HIGHLIGHTED

- Driving Force
- Selecting the Building
- Obtaining Local Authority Support
- Finding Appropriate Professionals
- Obtaining the Building on Good Terms
- Maintaining Financial Flexibility
- Using a Reliable Contractor
- Continuing Management

An example of a well-chosen scheme, where the building although in a run-down area was in sound condition and well suited for conversion into small units. From the start the development organisation was interested in managing the finished scheme and one driving force saw the project right the way through. In this case a non-profit Industrial Association was used as the development vehicle.

Key Facts

Original Building	Type:	Factory
	Construction:	Brick
	Date:	1863
	Size:	40,000 sq.ft.
	Storeys:	4 (plus basement)
	Location:	Near city centre
	Configuration:	Buildings around courtyards
	Condition:	Structurally sound
Concept	New Use:	Small Units (Studio/Office/Workshops)
	Developer:	Midlands Industrial Association
	Approach:	Entrepreneurial
	Manager:	Originator of scheme
Financing	Public Sector:	£151,000
	Private Sector:	£344,000
Devel-opment	Tenure:	Freehold
	Acquisition Cost:	£ 95,000
	Conversion Cost:	£395,000
	Date of Scheme:	1982–1984
	Lettable Area:	32,000 sq.ft.
	Cost per sq.ft. (gross):	£12.25 (1986 Equivalent: £13.20)*
	Cost per sq.ft. (net):	£15.30 (1986 Equivalent: £16.50)*
Result	No. of Units:	42 (Size Range 135 to 2273 sq.ft.)
	Employment:	157

*Adjusted for building cost inflation to approximate 1986 value

Figure 1 and 2: The Interior Courtyard during and after rehabilitation

PROJECT SUMMARY

The building
The Argent Centre is one of several attractive industrial buildings in Birmingham's former Jewellery Quarter, just to the north of the city centre. It is built of brick around three courtyards, with superb arched windows and fine ornamentation. The main part, dating from 1863, has four storeys and there are single storey additions, making a total of 40,000 sq.ft. The structure is strong and there is good access for lorries at one side.

The problem
Not only has Birmingham suffered typical inner city decay in the areas just outside the commercial centre, but also the whole West Midlands region, so long the powerhouse of British industry, has had a sharp economic decline, leaving many skilled people unemployed and many buildings empty. The previous owners of the Argent Centre, a large national company, rationalised its operations in 1982 and put the building up for sale.

The scheme
As large firms contracted, ways of encouraging small firms were sought. One approach to the provision of premises for small firms was through non-profit Industrial Associations, based on the Housing Association idea. Peter White of Midlands Industrial Association spotted the building, fell in love with it

and realised that by adding staircases and building partitions an exciting small business centre with attractive workspaces could be created.

The outcome
It took 18 months to put the scheme together and raise the finance, but the subsequent conversion went smoothly. A simple, all-in licence agreement was devised and the units were quickly let. Midlands Industrial Association has continued to manage the building with an occupancy rate of over 90%. The scheme has stimulated activity in the surrounding area and several buildings are being refurbished.

Figure 3: The arch windows provide plenty of natural light

ORGANISATION AND MANAGEMENT OF THE PROJECT

INCUBATION STAGE

Driving force

Undoubtedly Peter White was the driving force behind the Argent Centre. He saw it through all its stages. A planner by background, he had worked for several years as the development director of a Housing Association, but had become more and more interested in the creation of employment through small firms. In 1982 he helped to set up Midlands Industrial Association and gave up his secure job to run it. Not only did he spot the building originally and realise its potential, but he also helped draw up the plans and frequently visited the site during construction. He now manages the Argent Centre on behalf of Midlands and has his own office in it. He does not claim to have any particular qualities. He is just an ordinary person, but with determination, common sense and above all a real interest in making sure that the Argent Centre is a place where small businesses will flourish.

Organisation and objectives

Midlands Industrial Association Ltd. is a registered industrial and provident society (See p.31). It was established in association with North British Industrial Association, the pioneer in this field, but is now free-standing. Its aim is to act as a third force, between the public and private sectors, to encourage the growth of small businesses by providing and managing premises for them, in much the same way as Housing Associations have acted as a third force in the housing market.

The thinking behind Midlands was that by concentrating on one local economy, by choosing its projects carefully, by staying closely involved with its tenants (unlike a normal developer), by harnessing the enthusiasm of those who want small businesses to succeed, and by ploughing back all its profits it ought to become a powerful but trustworthy force in the promotion of small business. This philosophy coincided with Peter White's personal feelings. However, with no practical experience and feeling uncertain as to how to proceed he formed an alliance with North British Industrial Association, based in Preston, which was already established in this field. North British helped Midlands obtain a management contract from Birmingham City Council for one of their industrial estates, the Telsen Industrial Centre, which provided it with a basic income and experience in marketing and managing small units.

Selecting the building

Because of his local knowledge, Peter White came to hear that the Argent Centre building was for sale. He liked it immediately and felt it could become an ideal place for small firms. It was a wonderful building, in a central although run-down area, with plenty of natural light (see figure 3), good access and very little unuseable space. There was also scope for parking in the courtyards (see figures 1 and 2). Sealed bids for the freehold were required. From a back-of-the-envelope calculation he decided that the maximum that could be paid for the building was £90,000. On behalf of Midlands he put in an offer for this amount, conditional upon being able to raise the money, and it was accepted.

Finding appropriate professionals

Peter White did not know a suitable architect so he contacted one whose work he had seen nearby and liked. Through discussions it became clear that their ideas were very much in sympathy. Also the architect was happy to work with a builder whom Peter White had known in his Housing Association days and found to be very reliable. A quantity surveyor was later selected on the same basis.

Formulating the scheme

Although the main elements of the scheme were already clear in Peter White's mind, it took a further 18 months to put it all together. The architect worked out the basic scheme, and the builder in turn did the costings and made an estimate. The main works required were internal partitioning, electrical, plumbing, new lifts and staircases and a small amount of demolition to open up parts of the site. After allowing for the purchase of the building and for all professional and marketing fees, which voluntary organisations are apt to overlook, the total cost came to £465,000. The architect agreed to postpone his fees until the finance was raised.

Peter White and North British then put together a formal project proposal (in effect a Feasibility Study), documenting the shortage of suitable small units in Birmingham and estimating a rental income of just over £60,000 per year, allowing for voids, which would give an initial return of around 13% on £465,000. While an established institution might have been satisfied with this return, there was no way that Midlands Industrial Association which had no resources of its own could borrow all the money required. First, no private institution would be willing to finance all 100% of the costs and secondly, the income would only just cover the interest payments leaving nothing extra with which to start paying off the loan.

NEGOTIATION STAGE

Raising the finance

Midlands had good links with Birmingham City Council, who were pleased with the way it was managing the Telsen Industrial Centre and supported the proposed Argent Centre scheme. They advised that an application should be made for an Urban Development Grant, then a new part of the Urban Programme, so long as it could be shown that private sector finance amounting to two or three times the size of the grant would be available. Two major banks were approached, but turned the project down. Eventually, the Trustee Savings Bank, a traditionally small bank gearing itself up for a bigger future, agreed to advance two thirds of the money required, £307,000 on a 15-year loan at 2½% over base rate with repayments due to start after two years, provided that Birmingham City Council guaranteed the first two years' repayments. The Council not only agreed to do this but also strongly supported the grant application. Urban Development Grant of £151,400 was eventually approved.

Obtaining the building on good terms

Although Midlands' bid for the building had been accepted, raising the money took a long time. The banks were not very keen on an innovative project undertaken by an untried organisation, and sorting out the precise workings of Urban Development Grant caused further delay. The owners of the building were naturally anxious to be paid, and Peter White had to keep them from losing patience and cancelling their agreement. This he did by making friends with their surveyor and lawyers who were handling the sale and keeping them regularly informed of the progress that was being made. His enthusiasm for the project and his determination were infectious and the surveyor and lawyer became great allies. Eventually the building was bought a year and a half after the original offer for it had been made.

Maintaining financial flexibility

Because of the delays, costs rose. Interest rates increased and changes in the VAT laws imposed an additional and unforeseen burden. Midlands had virtually no funds of its own and so no financial flexibility. Costs rose by nearly £30,000 in spite of cut-backs to the original specification. Fortunately the previous owner of the building was happy to keep using one part of it for an extra year and agreed to pay £22,000 in rent, and so the extra money was found.

Sources of Finance

	£
Bank Loan	307,000
UDG (75% DoE)	113,550
(25% Birmingham City)	37,850
Rental Income etc.	31,600
	£490,000

Just as importantly, the management fees from the Telsen Centre enabled Midlands to keep its core team together during the long drawn out negotiations over the Argent Centre. The cost of doing this, although quite small and not strictly part of the costs of converting the Argent Centre, must not be forgotten.

Setting up a new project often takes a long time. Furthermore if a government grant is involved there is likely to be a delay between the submission of the fully worked out proposal and the payment of the grant (which usually cannot start until the next financial year). Survival during these early stages is a very real problem for new organisations. Midlands survived because its first project generated income.

CONSTRUCTION STAGE

Using a reliable contractor

The building work was carried out in two stages to suit the outgoing occupier. Although the basic structure was sound some alterations were required. The builder who had prepared the original estimates, and who had kept faith with the project in spite of the long delays, was employed as the single main contractor under a JCT contract (See p. 31). He was sufficiently experienced to be able to cope with the inevitable minor changes which became necessary as the work progressed. One of the main reasons why he had been selected in the first place was his known reliability.

Project management

Peter White remained as Project Manager even during the conversion work. The project architect supervised the contractor, but Peter White visited the site frequently and was able to see that everything went according to plan. Throughout the project Peter White and Midlands were interested in the future use of the building. The conversion work was merely a means to an end – helping the eventual tenants succeed by providing them with an exciting and supportive environment in which to work.

Keeping control of time and money

The quantity surveyor controlled the costs against the bill of quantities which had been included in the contract. He also prepared a simple bar chart to check that the main items of work were started and finished as planned. The standard of finish was functional and in no way lavish, but tenants were allowed to add their own finishing touches and special fittings if required.

MANAGEMENT STAGE

Marketing

With such a substantial debt burden overhanging the project it was obviously essential to market the space rapidly and to maintain a high level of occupancy. While the conversion work was still in progress an attractive brochure was circulated emphasising the points which from their previous management experience Midlands knew would be attractive to very small firms:–

- Small units
- Monthly terms
- Central location
- Parking, loading

- Reasonable rent
- Room for expansion
- Attractive building
- 24 hour access
- Security
- Office services

But over and above all these basic facilities there was Peter White's enthusiasm. He conveyed the feeling to prospective tenants that the Argent Centre was a good place for them to be. It catered specifically for small firms; it was going to be exciting and successful. A Minister from the Department of the Environment came to open it. There was favourable publicity for a local project in the local press. The initial space let very quickly, just as the Feasibility Study had predicted it would. Within one week of the building work finishing there were 16 tenants.

Continuing management

Midlands Industrial Association continues to own and manage the building. The second phase units also let immediately and there are now 42 units in total. Occupancy is around 90%, and this reflects the special atmosphere of the Argent Centre and the continuous energy which is put into management and marketing. Although no specific support is available to tenants, Peter White treats them as personal friends, is delighted with their successes and is always looking for ways to solve problems on their behalf. By being based in the building, he knows what is happening all the time and is able to ensure that adequate standards and the right atmosphere are maintained. Two part-time security and maintenance men are employed, so that any problems with the building can be rapidly put right. A 30,000 sq.ft. development is a good size to manage. Each tenant can be known individually, yet management costs are not excessive when spread over all units.

Although these informal relationships make all the difference, there is also a formal side to the management. Each occupier has a standard monthly licence, specifying exactly what has to be paid per month and requiring only one month's notice. Simple monthly forms keep track of occupancy and revenue unit by unit, and marketing activity is geared to the forecast level of vacancies. These statistics form the basis of a monthly report on performance to Midlands' Board. In contrast to a Housing Association, Board

Members are paid a small fee. This is felt to help attract good people to the Board, who treat it seriously and play an effective part. This prevents the manager from being too powerful or losing sight of the real objectives. The one dilemma facing the Association as a result of such a successful project is how quickly to try to go ahead with another scheme given that its borrowing capacity is still substantially tied up.

Notes

Industrial and provident society (IPS)

A non-profit organisation registered with the Registrar of Friendly Societies and incorporated under the Industrial and Provident Societies Act 1965, which must be either a bona fide co-operative or a business run for community benefit. Unlike an unincorporated friendly society, an IPS has limited liability which means that those who run it are not personally liable for its debts if things go wrong. Housing Associations are usually constituted this way.

JCT Contract

The most generally used form of contract for building works, under which the developer is responsible for the design, specification and supervision of the work and the contractor for carrying out the work as specified. It has standard clauses covering how payments are to be made, what happens (and who bears the costs) when changes occur, and many other eventualities.

Project references

PROJECT	Midlands Industrial Association Ltd.
ADDRESS	The Argent Centre, 60 Frederick Street, Birmingham B1 3HS Telephone: 021 233–2232
CONTACT	Peter White
PROJECT ARCHITECTS	Bonham Seager Associates Contact: Roger Seager, 94 Hagley Road, Birmingham B16 8NQ.

2 Curzon Street Station

Birmingham

Grade I Listed 19th Century Railway Station now re-used as headquarters for voluntary organisations. Local Authority development using public finance and an MSC scheme.

GOOD PRACTICES HIGHLIGHTED

- Driving Force
- Obtaining the Building on Good Terms
- Using an MSC Workforce
- Continuing Management

An example of how a historic building in poor condition, and with little prospect of viable commercial use, was rescued by a local authority at little cost to itself. Although no specific end-use was in mind at the start the local authority showed great commitment, and a viable re-use strategy was developed during the course of the project.

Key Facts

Original Building	*Type:*	Railway station
	Construction:	Stone
	Date:	1838
	Size:	9,700 sq.ft.
	Storeys:	3 (plus basement)
	Location:	Edge of city centre
	Configuration:	Square
	Condition:	Very poor
Concept	*New Use:*	Training organisation H.Q.
	Developer:	Birmingham City Council
	Approach:	Conservationist
	Manager:	Task Undertakings Ltd.
Finance	*Public Sector:*	£183,000
	Private Sector:	Nil
Development	*Tenure:*	Freehold
	Acquisition Cost:	£5,000 credit
	Conversion Cost:	£188,000 approx.
	Date of Scheme:	1979–1983
	Lettable Area:	6,520 sq.ft.
	Cost per sq.ft. (gross):	£19.00 (1986 Equivalent: £25.00)*
	Cost per sq.ft. (net):	£28.00 (1986 Equivalent: £37.00)*
Result	*No. of Units:*	Not relevant
	Employment:	80–100

*Adjusted for building cost inflation to approximate 1986 value

PROJECT SUMMARY

The building
Curzon Street Station was the original northern terminus of Stephenson's London and Birmingham Railway. Built in 1838 it is a small but imposing Grade I listed building, intended to match the Euston Arch at the other end of the line. It has striking Ionic columns outside and a large central hall within, which runs right up to the roof and takes up much of the internal space. There is a fine staircase, with galleries round the hall leading to suites of rooms.

The problem
In 1852 a new passenger station was opened at New Street and Curzon Street became a goods depot, which did not need a fine building and booking hall. Eventually the building fell into complete disuse. In 1970, and again in 1978, Listed Building Consent to demolish it was sought, but refused. By this time the roof was in very poor condition and the building was infested with dry rot. Recognising that it was less than worthless, British Rail donated it in 1979 to Birmingham City Council along with £5,000. Because of its design it had only a relatively small amount of usable floor space, and could not be economically redeveloped in a conventional manner.

The scheme
The City Council immediately spent £22,000 to make the building wind and water tight. They then obtained MSC and DoE funding to renovate the building completely, using temporarily unemployed labour. The work was initially organised by the City Council itself and subsequently taken on by Task Undertakings, a non-profit job creation and training agency.

The outcome
The building was restored to a high standard and Task Undertakings were delighted to take it on and use it as

Figure 5: Task Undertakings converted and use the restored Curson Street Station

Figure 4: Fine architectural detail was restored to its original state

their own headquarters. Thus a fine building was saved from decay and from being a public liability without the local authority having to spend too much of its own money.

Organisation and management of the project

INCUBATION STAGE

Driving force
The restoration of Curzon Street Station was initiated by Graham Shaylor, City Planning Officer of Birmingham City Council, and the Planning Department masterminded the project. Furthermore there was a driving force who had an interest in the scheme right through to its end use. David Chapman was a member of the Planning Department team which put together the original case for saving the building, he acted as Project Architect and later he was allowed to take 3½ years leave to become a director of Task Undertakings Ltd., the MSC-sponsored organisation which did much of the restoration and rebuilding work and eventually occupied Curzon Street Station as its headquarters.

During this time he was not only concerned with the building works and the training of the workforce, but also managed to ensure that there was a suitable use for the restored building. He thus turned a building project into a scheme with a viable end-use and ensured its successful conclusion. He subsequently rejoined the Planning Department.

Objectives

The City Council's original objective was to save the building without having to spend a fortune on it themselves. The idea of organising a conservation project to train people in building skills while they helped rebuild it was clever and took advantage of the MSC's need to find training opportunities for young people. The MSC paid the wages of all the trainees and their supervisors. Little thought was originally given to the future use of the building. Clearly, since so much public money had been spent on it, it could not be put to a purely private use. The eventual idea of Task Undertakings using the building as its own headquarters encouraged those working on the scheme to take extra pride in their work and make it a success. Thus, in the end, the use did become an important part of the scheme. The building is now viable and does not require any further spending by the City Council.

Selecting the building

The building selected itself. British Rail had a Grade I listed building (see p. 37) which they were not interested in. They took their problem to the City Council. At that time there were two other listed buildings whose future was in serious jeopardy. The City Council decided to take on all three, including Curzon Street Station. The idea was to restore the buildings architecturally (see figure 4) and then find a sensible use for them. This project therefore started with the building.

Formulating the scheme

No detailed feasibility study was undertaken. The City Council decided to take responsibility for a historic building, and to spend a modest sum on making it safe and preventing further deterioration ('mothballing' it).

They then looked for a way of refurbishing it at minimum cost to themselves, and decided on an MSC training project. They then looked for a use for the building which would keep it in running order without costing the Council anything and which would not conflict with the investment of public funds in the restoration. This rather leisurely approach to formulating a scheme contrasts sharply with what is required in most conversion schemes. In this case the building was practically free, and so no justifications had to be made after the initial decision, so long as the building was restored and re-used.

The Planning Department masterminded the scheme. At the outset they had to convince the Planning and Highways Committee that the Council should take responsibility for the building, but thereafter the department had a free hand. The Council's own professional staff prepared the drawings and specifications, and the Planning Department used its organising ability – and their ability to get advice from other Council departments – to set up and oversee the project.

NEGOTIATION STAGE

Obtaining the building on good terms

When British Rail gave the building to the Council they also gave a grant of £5,000. While this understated the problem (the Council had to spend a further £17,000 in making the building watertight) it was at least a recognition of the fact that the building had a negative value. This is all too often the case with large redundant buildings, which makes conventional asset-related financing of conversion projects difficult, and underlines the importance of government grants.

Even so, in this instance, it might have been better if the Council had insisted on British Rail making more land around the building available in order to improve access and parking. One of the first things that had to be done on this scheme was to demolish a hotel, which was a later addition to the building, in order to provide parking space.

Raising the finance

To start with the Council spent £22,000 on securing the building, £5,000 coming from British Rail and £17,000 from its own resources. The Council used its own money because this work had to be done without delay in order to prevent further deterioration of the building. For the main restoration work, however, there was no particular hurry, and it made sense to apply for grants. The two most obvious sources of funds were the Manpower Services Commission (MSC) (see p. 37), which could pay the salaries of people employed on approved schemes, and the Department of the Environment (DoE).

The Planning Department succeeded in obtaining MSC funding for a three year 12-place workforce and an allowance of £25,000 for materials. They also obtained an £85,000 grant from the DoE under its Operation Clean-up scheme (which has since been absorbed into the Urban Programme). The City Council had to meet 25% of this grant itself. In addition, the Council paid a small amount for materials and provided support from its in-house professionals. It is estimated that this amounted to £51,000.

Sources of Finance

	£
Birmingham City Council	89,000
DoE-Operation Clean-Up	63,000
MSC – Materials Allowance	25,000
British Rail	5,000
MSC – Salaries	Nil*
	£183,000

*So far as project was concerned

Maintaining flexibility

Being totally public funded the scheme lacked flexibility. This has sometimes proved a problem on MSC schemes where it is not always easy to predict schedules and efficiencies. In practice the scheme took longer than originally anticipated. However this did not particularly matter to the City Council. Nor did it matter to Task Undertakings. Its role was to organise employment and training for a given number of people, rather than to carry out a specific project within a specified period. It was therefore quite pleased to extend the work period on Curzon Street to generate more employment. This provided one form of flexibility.

However, as on many large conversion schemes, unpredicted work requiring materials as well as labour was discovered long after the original estimates were made. In this case structural repairs were required; the dry rot had progressed further than anticipated and when the building was finally reused some of the drains were found to be deficient. While some of this could be covered by juggling within overall cash limits, the Council were able to find small amounts of extra money when needed. Also the support and effort put in by the local authority team, which may not have been fully reflected in the fees charged, made a great contribution to the scheme and provided additional flexibility.

CONSTRUCTION STAGE

Project management

David Chapman, the planner originally responsible for the Curzon Street Station project, had a wider personal interest in urban and employment regeneration. He was granted leave of absence to help establish Task Undertakings, whose brief was to set up and manage projects on which unemployed people in the Birmingham area could find temporary jobs. Curzon Street Station became Task Undertaking's first project, and so David Chapman had a particular interest in ensuring the success of both. It was far-sighted and generous of the Council to release him and especially fortunate for this project. Furthermore, when Task Undertakings began to grow into a substantial organisation (it now provides employment and training for over 1000 people), it needed its own administrative offices and training workshops. Where better to be located than in a building which it had converted itself? David Chapman was able to propose Curzon Street Station as Task Undertakings' headquarters, and thus, with the MSC paying a reasonable rent, ensure a viable future for it.

Although David Chapman's dual role was unusual, it does illustrate the advantages of having, by whatever means, someone with a real stake in the sustainable re-use of the building in charge of the project and of having good links between a project and the local authority.

Using an MSC workforce

Task Undertakings acted as an arm's length contractor and was very keen to do a good job. Many developers, including voluntary groups, are reluctant to use MSC workforces because of the difficulty in organising them and the fear of inadequate results. There is, however, the alternative of using established Managing Agents (see p. 37), some of which have built up considerable experience and expertise and can offer a track record of good quality. Where the objectives of the scheme permit it, it could be well worth seeing if there is an MSC Managing Agent capable of undertaking a proposed conversion project.

In this case the MSC workforce, then working under the Special Temporary Employment Programme which has now been superseded by the Community Programme, did an excellent job. Indeed the Curzon Street Station is now a showpiece of what can be done by an MSC workforce. The main difficulty encountered was that of recruiting good supervisors, who play a vital role because of the inexperience of the workforce. They, too, had to be recruited from among the unemployed and could only stay on the project for one year. Finding replacements was a constant headache. They are now allowed to stay for up to two years.

There was some skilled masonry work which Task Undertakings could not then do. It was subcontracted separately to a firm of stone-masons. This caused no problem, and Task Undertakings now reckon that they have sufficient experience to tackle most specialist work.

Keeping control of time and money

Task Undertakings took responsibility for managing the work just as any normal contractor would do. The Council's professional team were responsible for checking that the work was being done to the required standard and that the correct amounts of materials were being used. Control of time was not so important.

MANAGEMENT STAGE

Continuing management

A number of voluntary groups and charities showed interest in taking space in the suites of rooms provided by the restoration. The building was prestigious and close to the centre of the city. No marketing had to be done. Although the Council did not need to earn a high rent from the building they wanted to ensure that it would be well managed and generate sufficent income to cover all running costs and maintenance. For this reason it was desirable for the tenants, or at least the principal tenant, to have the backing of a substantial body. Task Undertakings itself, with its backing from the MSC, was the most suitable potential tenant and it now uses most of the building for offices, design studios and joinery and metal workshops (see figure 5). It also manages the building. Other tenants include the Prince's Trust and Access-for-All, a disabled people's pressure group. Curzon Street Station has therefore been given new life without the need of permanent subsidy from the City Council.

Notes

Listed Buildings

Buildings of special architectural or historic interest are listed by the Historic Buildings Division of the DoE, and formal Listed Building Consent is required before any alteration, extension or demolition can take place. The list is divided into three categories:

Grade II   Buildings of Special Architectural or Historic Interest

Grade II*   Particularly Important Buildings in Grade II

Grade I   Buildings of National Importance

There are about 300,000 listed buildings in England, but fewer than 6,000 are Grade I.

Manpower Services Commission (MSC)

The government agency with responsibility for training and employment creation. The Community Programme is a temporary employment scheme under which the MSC pays wages and other costs, up to set limits, to enable the long term unemployed to work on community projects that would not otherwise be done. A Managing Agent administers a number of projects under a contract with the MSC.

Project references

PROJECT ADDRESS	Curzon Street Station, 1 Curzon Street, Birmingham B4 7XG. Telephone: 021 359–2862
CONTACT	Reg Elmer, Task Undertakings Ltd.
PROJECT ARCHITECTS	Development Department, Birmingham City Council, 120 Edmund Street, Birmingham B3 2RD Contact: David Chapman

3   Dean Clough Industrial Park

Halifax, West Yorkshire

Huge 19th Century textile mill, now re-used as an industrial estate for small firms with many public and private support services. Private development, privately financed.

GOOD PRACTICES HIGHLIGHTED

- Driving Force
- Entrepreneurial Approach
- Selecting the Building
- Formulating the Scheme
- Obtaining Local Authority Support
- Maintaining Flexibility
- Marketing
- Continuing Management

An astonishing example of how an entrepreneur took on a vast empty mill in the depths of recession and, by reacting to opportunities, turned it into a thriving industrial estate – mostly for small firms. This was done without any direct public or institutional investment.

Key Facts

Original Building	*Type:*	Textile Mill
	Construction:	Stone
	Date:	1840
	Size:	1,250,000 sq.ft.
	Storeys:	1 to 10
	Location:	Near town centre
	Configuration:	Long, narrow buildings
	Condition:	Structurally sound
Concept	*New Use:*	Small Units & services
	Developer:	Private individual
	Approach:	Entrepreneurial
	Manager:	Owner and son
Finance	*Public Sector:*	None
	Private Sector:	Not available
Development	*Tenure:*	Freehold
	Acquisition Cost	Not available
	Conversion Cost:	Not available
	Date of Scheme:	1983 onwards
	Lettable Area:	600,000 sq.ft. (so far)
	Cost per sq.ft. (net):	£2.00 (basic space)* to £15.00 (office/studio)* £20.00 (small offices)*
Result	*No. of Units:*	140 (and increasing)
	Employment:	900

*Adjusted for building cost inflation to approximate 1986 value

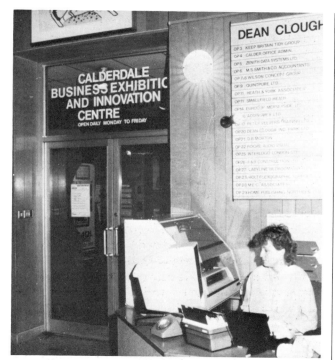

Figure 6: Dean Clough now houses Calderdale's Business, Exhibition and Innovation Centre.

PROJECT SUMMARY

The building
Dean Clough is a complex of multi-storied granite buildings – 1.25 million sq.ft. in all – in the centre of Halifax. It was previously the headquaters of a carpet manufacturing company that declined sharply in the 1970's leaving the buildings empty, although structurally sound.

The problem
The problems were size and location, a massive empty mill in the centre of the town, in a region that already contained 10 million sq.ft. of empty industrial property. The local authority had reluctantly concluded demolition was the only answer.

The scheme
Ernest Hall bought Dean Clough because he saw it as an opportunity; an opportunity to create an exciting working environment with supporting cultural, educational and leisure activities. Its size would increase impact and excitement. Its central location would be good for tenants and their customers. His idea was to provide premises and if needed business advice for small firms, especially start-ups. He was convinced that, with a little initial support, many people could run their own businesses. As the number of tenants increased he would be able to attract in more services, both public and private, and build up a culture of success. Not only would he have the challenge of carrying through an exciting scheme, but he would also end up with a very valuable asset.

The outcome
Within 3 years there were over 140 tenants, including all the main local agencies supporting small businesses, an art gallery and a thriving pub/restaurant. Over 600,000 sq.ft. were occupied. More people were at work in the buildings than in the old carpet factory and triple the amount of rates were being paid. In cash terms the scheme had reached break even, and there was a definite air of success.

Organisation and management of the project

INCUBATION STAGE

Driving force
The clear, individual driving force behind Dean Clough Industrial Park has been Ernest Hall. He is an unassuming person, but has plenty of energy and

Figure 7: Quality of finish varies greatly; a basic unit.

Figure 8: Reuse on demand from clients

enthusiasm. He has a track record of success both as a concert pianist and as a businessman. He founded and built up his own multi-million pound textile company before selling out in 1983. He is universally described as an entrepreneur, someone who is able to take advantage of business opportunities and to solve problems. He says of himself that it often takes him a long time to work out the right solution, but he can always tell when he has found it – it is so simple and obvious.

Objectives

Ernest Hall's objectives at Dean Clough were both personal and commercial. From the outset he had a strong concept of what he wanted to create, an environment in which education, culture and recreation would complement work; a special place with a culture of success in which small businesses could grow, gain confidence and prosper. Not only would he enjoy creating this, but it would also be profitable and would help revive the local economy. He would benefit from the success of his tenants, without having to take on too much risk or hassle, and if he succeeded in creating the right environment, there would never be a shortage of tenants in spite of the size of the building. Everyone wants to join in a success.

Entrepreneurial approach

Ernest Hall is a developer of people. He believes that most people can achieve more than they think they can, and he feels that he can often recognise business potential and help it succeed. This is what Dean Clough is all about. The conversion of the buildings was a means to a definite end, and Ernest Hall clearly took an entrepreneurial approach to development. He had a definite idea of the type of activity and atmosphere that he wished to generate but was flexible and pragmatic in achieving it.

> **'All I've done here is to have the flexibility to respond dynamically to other people and to the exciting opportunities that keep coming up'**

This in turn led to a phased approach, and after three years only about half the space had been converted. Furthermore he and his son Jeremy are fully committed to the scheme and are involved full time in its management and continuing development. He has also been prepared to invest in a limited way in some of the businesses at Dean Clough by charging low rents initially and by giving advice and support, but tenants are expected to earn enough profit to pay a proper rent within a reasonable period of time.

> **'I don't mind helping your business get off the ground, but why should I be subsidising your customers who I don't even know? Go off and charge them a proper price and make your business profitable.'**

Selecting the building

Within limits any large building would have been suitable. It had to be large to enable a mixed community to develop, but it did not have to be as big as 1.25 million sq.ft. It had to be cheap and in sound condition, so as to limit financial exposure in case the whole project failed. It had to be accessible and have good access. It had to be simple to subdivide into different types and sizes of space, each with plenty of natural light.

Dean Clough fitted all these criteria. It was so large that it was thought most unlikely that a buyer would be found for it. It was therefore cheap, and certainly far cheaper than any new building of comparable size would have been. Ernest Hall liked the buildings and knew intuitively that his ideas could work there. The buildings looked sound and had been in recent use, so he did not bother with a survey. He did not undertake any feasibility study. He consulted no professionals, except his solicitor. He knew that there was plenty of cheap space available in West Yorkshire with rents of around £1 per sq.ft. It was obvious to him that, even at those levels, the project would be viable if he let a reasonable portion of the space, and he was sure that there would be a demand for his space once he could demonstrate it to be a success. He therefore bought the buildings, insisting on a freehold as he was investing for the long term.

Formulating the scheme

While he already knew in outline what he was planning to do, the exact details of the scheme evolved step by step as he went along. He started by advertising, to attract the attention of potential tenants, and by offering the space that could be occupied immediately at reasonable rents. Virtually anybody who wanted space, except those who might blight the site, was accepted and within a year there were 70 tenants employing over 400 people. As more tenants moved in, more office service companies were persuaded to move in to serve them. The success of Dean Clough could then be publicised and yet more firms invited to come and join in.

At the same time efforts were made to attract in tenants, at preferential rents if necessary, who would add particular value to the Dean Clough community such as a wine bar, a restaurant, an art gallery and a theatre company, as well as a whole range of local institutions whose activities could help to foster small businesses including:–

- Calderdale Business Exhibition Centre (see figure 6)
- Enterprise Training Services
- Calderdale Small Business Advice Centre
- Calderdale Chamber of Commerce
- Manpower Services Commission Regional Office
- EEC Business and Innovation Centre.

The tenants would benefit from having all these services close at hand, and this in turn would attract more tenants. The message was:–

> **We are creating something exciting here. It is like putting together pieces of a jigsaw. Enormous failure is turning into enormous success. Don't you want to join in? You'll work better here?**

The approach was thus opportunistic and incremental. It was not a case of doing the conversion first and then looking for tenants, but the exact opposite: start by bringing in tenants and income straight away, and then gradually convert more and more of the building as demand increases. Thus the scheme was formulated piecemeal as it went along, taking advantage of opportunities as they came and keeping a balance between income and investment in the building. Not every idea worked out in practice, but most did and those that did not were dropped.

Obtaining local authority support

Although he was not planning to apply for any grants, Ernest Hall made sure that the local authority, Calderdale Borough Council, supported the scheme right from the outset. He has deliberately built up good personal relations with the Council. They in turn took a positive attitude over planning and building regulations, and only charged rates on the parts of the buildings that were actually occupied. Rates can have an important impact on the economics of partially occupied buildings (See p. 43).

NEGOTIATION STAGE

Raising the finance

Ernest Hall used his own money to buy and develop Dean Clough. He wanted to be free to do things his way, to support tenants as he wished, to develop Dean Clough at the speed he felt appropriate. He did not set out to make a normal developer's return immediately, but he had every intention of making the buildings generate income from the start. It would have been possible for him to apply for Urban Development Grant or a grant from the European Regional Development Fund, but both these would have involved relatively long application times and commitment to a building timetable which would have removed some of his flexibility. He might have raised some private institutional finance, but the project itself had little security to offer, nor did it offer the rapid returns of normal property development. The type of finance that he needed was venture capital, as like any entrepreneur he was founding a whole new business. Such money is not easy to find, it was simplest to provide it himself.

Details of the amounts of money spent on the scheme are not available. It is likely however that over £1 million has been invested, and while few people could afford such a sum, it is quite possible for others to follow this example on a smaller scale. Buying for around £1 per sq.ft., converting for £3–£4 and renting for £1 per sq.ft. per year, as described in Roger Tym's *Mills in the 80's* (21) is quite feasible. Dean Clough is not unrepeatable.

Maintaining flexibility

Flexibility has been the keynote of the Dean Clough project. The buildings were large enough to provide a whole range of different types of space and, with no pressures due to capital grants having to be spent in particular financial years, the conversion work could be undertaken in line with demand (figures 7 and 8). In this way the amount of unlet converted space has been kept to a minimum and cash inflow and cash outflows have been more nearly balanced, for it is unlet converted space that represents the real financial risk in a conversion scheme. Flexibility has thus been used to reduce risk.

Finding appropriate professionals

Professions have not been greatly used on this project partly because the building work has been undertaken as many small assignments and partly as Ernest Hall believes that the crucial jobs should not be delegated except to someone who can clearly do a better job. Responsibility for the scheme must remain with the driving force.

> **'Professionals have their uses, but they don't normally have the time to think out your problem deeply enough. Do your own thinking. Use your own judgement . . . For example, I do all the negotiations with the Building Regulations people myself, for I know they are vital'**

CONSTRUCTION STAGE

Project management

A considerable amount of building work has been undertaken, but it has been done as a series of small projects as different parts of different buildings have been brought back into re-use. Most of the work has involved partitioning, installing services, fire proofing and upgrading the finishes. Some spaces have been let in a very basic condition, others have been converted to a high standard. There is room for an enormous range at Dean Clough.

The underlying thinking about each project is done by Ernest Hall. A local architect-designer produces the detailed specifications. Local subcontractors quote for and carry out the various parts of the work. Jeremy Hall acts as Project Manager and oversees the work done, usually checking on progress every day. Some of the firms have now worked on several projects; their reliability is known and they are easier to supervise. As Jeremy and Ernest Hall work closely together and are on the site full time there is no problem of ensuring that the driving force's vision is being put into effect.

Keeping control of time and money

Sophisticated controls are not required to oversee the building works. Control is mainly exercised by being on the spot. Each subcontractor will have normally quoted a fixed price for his work, and so over-runs are unusual. Ultimately all expenditure comes out of

Ernest Hall's pocket and there is no control more direct than actually having to write out the cheques.

Where several subcontractors have to be co-ordinated, it is important to keep control over time. Again this is done on a personal basis. Each subcontractor is kept aware of when each piece of work is expected to start and to finish and any problems over scheduling can be resolved by discussion on site. Working with the same firms makes the anticipation and solving of problems easier, and it is the job of the Project Manager to ensure that everything knows what is expected of them and is working to the same timetable.

MANAGEMENT STAGE

Marketing

The objective of the scheme was to create and sustain a culture of success. This has required careful management and Ernest Hall has had to remain fully involved. Marketing has been extremely important and has had two aims, to attract in businesses as tenants, and to attract in the public and other support services. Publicity, especially through the local press, has been the main way of attracting tenants, and a great deal of effort has been put into it. The single message has been that of 'success', success at Dean Clough which others can join in. Attracting the public services has required direct personal contact and persuasion. Again this is a role that only the driving force can carry through, and Ernest Hall has usually found that, by combining other people's ideas (for example, for a Business and Innovation Centre) with his own, both sets of objectives can often be achieved – at Dean Clough.

Continuing management

The management is in the hand of Ernest and Jeremy Hall. With so many people working in a relatively confined space, direct 'hands-on' management is required. But efficient estate management is not enough, and by itself would not maintain Dean Clough's momentum. So Ernest Hall continues to provide advice and support to tenants, either directly or through the Enterprise Training Service; a new exhibition is organised in the modern art gallery every few weeks, and seminars, exhibitions and other events are frequently held. New projects are always being developed in order to keep up the feeling of activity and progress.

Established firms are starting to take space in Dean Clough, which is now widely acknowledged as a success. It offers almost everything that a new building could offer, but is much cheaper. In 3 years a huge, redundant and almost worthless building has been shown to be a great asset.

Notes

Rating of partially occupied buildings

Since April 1984 empty industrial buildings have been exempt from rates. But once any space is used it is liable for full rates. Care must therefore be taken to ensure that the parts of a large building that are capable of being occupied separately are rated separately (by the Inland Revenue's Valuation Officer), so that the exemption can be claimed on the parts which are not occupied.

Project references

PROJECT ADDRESS	Dean Clough Industrial Park Ltd., Halifax HX3 5AX Telephone: 0422–44555
CONTACT	Ernest Hall, Chairman
PROJECT ARCHITECTS	Morton Design Consultants, Dean Clough

4   Imperial Studios

Imperial Road, London SW6

A former bus depot, now re-used as small workshop, office and studio units for high technology firms. Developed by a property company, using private and public money including Urban Programme loan.

GOOD PRACTICES HIGHLIGHTED

- Driving Force

- Formulating the Scheme

- Obtaining Local Authority Support

- Raising the Finance

A profitable conversion by conventional but innovative property developers. The local authority played a crucial role by actively supporting the scheme and providing pump priming finance, as the scheme appeared too risky for the private sector. However a pioneering property fund did buy the completed development enabling the conventional approach to pay off. Also an illustration of how highly professional developers settle all the details of a scheme, and shed most of the risks, before committing themselves.

Key Facts

Original Building	Type:	Garage
	Construction:	Steel frame and brick
	Date:	1930
	Size:	22,000 sq.ft. (gross)
	Storeys:	1
	Location:	Inner city
	Configuration:	Long and thin
	Condition:	Poor
Concept	New Use:	Studio and workshop units
	Developer:	Small development company
	Approach:	Conventional
	Manager:	Sold to property unit trust
Finance	Public Sector:	£200,000 loan
	Private Sector:	£260,000
Development	Tenure:	Freehold
	Acquisition Cost:	£250,000
	Conversion Cost:	£210,000
	Date of Scheme:	
	Lettable Area:	20,200 sq.ft.
	Cost per sq.ft. (gross):	£21.00 (1986 Equivalent: £24.00)*
	Cost per sq.ft. (net):	£23.30 (1986 Equivalent: £25.50)*
Result	No. of Units:	23
	Employment:	80

*Adjusted for building cost inflation to approximate 1986 value

PROJECT SUMMARY

The building
Originally a vehicle workshop and garage belonging to North Thames Gas, Imperial Studios was basically a long, low, single storey shed giving access directly onto the road. It was located in Fulham in inner South West London, next to an enormous gas works and on the edge of a run-down industrial area. In 1982 it was being used as a bus depot.

The problem
Large industrial concerns were continuing to move out of inner London and there was little use for the premises they left behind. Conventional property wisdom said that they would remain empty or in low grade use until there was a strong upsurge in the economy. Others believed that there could be demand for high quality units for small firms, especially near residential areas. Someone had to take a risk and see.

The scheme
The Bourne brothers were property developers who had very specific ideas as to the type of tenant for whom they wished to provide premises. They wanted to cater for small high tech/design firms, the 'quiet industries' whose presence would enhance either residential or industrial areas. Imperial Road seemed to them an ideal location and the building could be subdivided into a range of small units, but first the finance and then the tenants had to be found. Private sector finance was not forthcoming until the local council, which strongly supported the scheme, provided a loan through the Urban Programme.

The outcome
23 very attractive units were created. All were let within a few weeks and the finished scheme was sold on to a small property fund. It proved the existence of demand from small firms and the developers have gone on to many other projects. Furthermore the area around Imperial Studios has since greatly improved with investment in both housing and industrial units.

Organisation and management of the project

INCUBATION STAGE

Driving force
Imperial Studios was developed by the Local London Group, a small development company, which has specialised in providing offices and workspaces for small firms. It was owned and run by two brothers, Robert Bourne, a chartered accountant, and Graham Bourne, a surveyor. They were in their mid-thirties and worked together very efficiently. Although they had always wanted to work together they had deliberately gained experience in their respective fields before founding the Local London Group. Between them they had property and financial deal making skills, and the both had drive. They were the driving force behind Imperial Studios.

Objectives
The Bourne brothers were property developers. Profit was their first objective. But they also reckoned that their small scale developments would bring benefits to the local community, by providing employment near where people lived and by introducing high environmental standards. They were among the first professional developers to cater for the small business sector, and their ideas have gained increasing support.

Selecting the building
The Bourne brothers operated primarily in south west London. They had done developments in Hammersmith and Fulham before. They were constantly on the look out for new opportunities and in the Spring of 1982 they came across a site in Imperial Road which

Figure 9: Parking and easy access is a basic requirement well met at Imperial.

Figure 10: Clean, functional lines of the new units with large doors for access.

was being used as a bus depot. They checked and found that it was on a register of vacant and under-used commercial property kept by Hammersmith and Fulham's Economic Development Unit. Its owners, the Gas Board, were interested in selling. Although the building was in a very bad state, the Bourne brothers thought it had great potential. Its location was right, being on a main road (soon to be widened), on the fringe of a residential area and within easy reach of central London. Also it was a single storey building with a long frontage on the road and capable of being divided easily into small units (figure 9).

Formulating the scheme

Thus the Bourne brothers were already moving quickly even before the building had come onto the market. They already knew what they wanted and they kept looking for buildings that could provide it. The Imperial Road depot seemed to fit and to be available at a reasonable price, and so they decided to work up a detailed conversion scheme and a detailed financing proposal.

Finding appropriate professionals

Knowing that architects and builders were short of work, they approached several and asked them to design in outline and cost schemes that would meet their specific requirements. The scheme by builders Dickson-Howe Contracts Ltd. and their architect, Alain Bouvier, was preferred. It was an exciting design, and because the roof height was 20 feet in the centre of the building there was room for a mezzanine floor. However the architect decided to make two storeys only in a small central section which provided a number of very small units of around 400 sq.ft. with their own reception area and shared facilities. Most of the other units were just left as single 1100 sq.ft. units, but with the marketing carrot that if the tenants wished to expand they could easily add their own mezzanine

Obtaining local authority support

The Local London Group was already in contact with the local authority before the scheme began, as it was already developing a business centre for small firms in another part of the borough. Hammersmith and Fulham was regarded as one of the pioneers in the field of local economic development and members of its Economic Development Unit were already familiar with the Bourne brothers' approach and approved of it. One of their functions is to play a positive, enabling role to help approved schemes succeed in the borough. They strongly supported the Imperial Studios scheme and worked closely with the professional team. One particular problem which had to be over-come was parking and loading as there was no free space on the site. With the co-operation of the various council departments a solution was found. The units were provided with internal parking space, with entry through large opening doors, though everyone knew that cars might park outside (figure 10).

Meanwhile the Local London Group carried out its own market survey to establish that the type of design/high tech tenants that it was seeking to attract would be interested in Imperial Studios at the rents they hoped to charge.

NEGOTIATION STAGE

Obtaining the building on good terms

The Bourne brothers were only interested in obtaining the freehold of the site. This would make it much easier to raise money for the conversion using the property as security, and easier to sell the completed scheme afterwards. They had dealt with the Gas Board previously, which made the negotiations easier and a price of £250,000 was agreed, subject to the finance being available.

Raising the finance

In all nearly £500,000 was required. The Bourne brothers approached several banks, but owing to the Local London Group's short track record and to the preceived riskiness of the project, none would lend unless there was another significant investment first. Hammersmith and Fulham's Economic Development Unit was able to help once again. It had an established programme, called the 'Small Workshops Rolling Programme', for lending money under the Urban Programme to suitable development projects. Under this scheme the Borough Council was able to borrow money for approved projects, with the Department of the Environment contributing 75% of the loan charges, and then lend it on to the project on a long term basis.

The Economic Development Unit felt that a pump priming loan, rather than an outright grant, was the best way of using public funds in support of a private, profit-seeking development.

By law the Borough Council had to have adequate security for the loan. However it was prepared to take a second mortgage, leaving the first mortgage (or the first claim on the value of the building) to the banks so as to encourage them to lend. The Council's own Valuation Department could not put a figure on the value of the proposed development because they had nothing to compare it with. An experienced outside firm, Jones Lang Wootton, were called in and they gave an estimate of £550,000, which effectively set the ceiling on the amount that could be borrowed. In the event this turned out to be a very conservative estimate, but if the project had gone wrong and the building fetched a price significantly below the valuer's estimate they might have become liable to pay compensation for the difference. For this reason professional valuers tend to be cautious, which does not help innovative schemes.

However with a valuation of £550,000, Hammersmith and Fulham were prepared to apply to the DoE for approval of a £200,000 loan (to be made under s. 2 of the Inner Urban Areas Act, 1978). Approval was given and the Council made a 25-year loan to the Local London Group at ¼% above their own borrowing rate, which at that time was some 4% below the rate which the Group had to pay on the private sector borrowings. As soon as this was arranged, bank loans of £250,000 to buy the building were approved, and the project went ahead with very little money required from the Bourne brothers themselves.

Sources of finance

	£
Bank Loan	250,000
UP-Funded Loan	200,000
Own Resources	10,000
	£460,000

Maintaining financial flexibility

Ultimately any financial flexibility would have had to have been provided by the Bourne brothers themselves, but they took steps to reduce the uncertainties. They were prepared to take the marketing risks. Marketing was their responsibility. If tenants were not obtained at the right time or at the right rent, they would bear the loss. However the builders would take the risk on the costs of conversion. The building contract would be a design and build contract (see p. 49), with penalty clauses for delays. The architect even delayed the start of the building contract by a month while costings were revised in detail so as to avoid on-site problems and revisions. All subcontracts were made fixed price too. Thus the need for flexibility was reduced and everybody, builders, architect, developer, bankers and the Council, had a keen interest in getting the project finished within budget and on time.

With the help of the Urban Programme loan, the Bourne brothers had now made an innovative scheme, of the type that had usually been done previously by 'amateur' developers, fit into the conventional development formula. Before the building work had even started they began approaching property funds with a view to selling on the completed and tenanted scheme. One of the main factors which had dissuaded conventional developers from being involved in the provision of small units was the reluctance of the financial institutions which traditionally invest in property (such as pension funds and insurance companies) to buy and manage small units. In 1982, however, a new fund called The London Small Business Property Trust (see p. 49) formed for the very purpose of filling this gap, and it agreed to acquire the completed scheme at a pre-arranged multiple of the rental income achieved.

CONSTRUCTION STAGE

Project management

Responsibility for the construction stage was entirely in the hands of the architect and the contractors, working to a tight schedule. The Local London Group acted as their own project managers and took a close interest in all that was done so as to help sort out any problems as they arose. They employed independent quantity surveyors, Donaldson's, to check the building certificates before releasing funds. But, freed from the necessity of directly supervising the building work they got on with the task of marketing. They also kept all the interested parties informed as to progress so as to maintain confidence in and enthusiasm for the scheme. As soon as the conversion work permitted it, the Local London Group set up an office in Imperial Studios, ostensibly to do the marketing, but it also enabled them to be aware of everything that was happening and to make any necessary decisions on the spot.

Keeping control of time and money

By having negotiated fixed contracts with penalty clauses, control of time and money became the sole responsibility of the contractors. At the end they worked 24 hours a day, 7 days a week, to complete the contract on time. By having all the details of the scheme agreed and costed in advance there was little need for specification changes as the work progressed, and indeed these were largely limited to specific requests from confirmed tenants.

Dealing with the unexpected

Although the whole scheme took 18 months, the construction work took only 6 months. The first year had been spent sorting out all the details in advance. This highly professional approach paid off and the construction stage went quickly and smoothly.

MANAGEMENT STAGE

Marketing

As the development had already been sold in advance the only remaining task was to let the units at the desired rents (£6 to 8.50 per sq.ft.) to tenants who fitted in with the aims of the scheme. An attractive brochure was produced emphasising the good location, the parking facilities and the possibility of expansion. The estate agents who were to manage the property on behalf of the London Small Business Property Trust were retained to help sell the units and the Local London Group set up its own office in the building.

The demand which the Bourne brothers had anticipated existed, and the finished scheme itself looked very attractive. All the units were quickly let and the sale of the development concluded. Since then there has been more investment in the other buildings and sites around Imperial Studios and the whole area is beginning to improve.

Notes

Design and build contract

A type of building contract under which the contractor takes responsibility not only for the construction work but also for its design and the specification. The developer prepares a **performance specification** which sets out the precise requirements for the building and the contractor commits to meeting those requirements, usually at a fixed price. The contractor employs the architect and takes a substantial share of the development risk (and is likely to make allowance for this in the price).

The London Small Business Property Trust was formed in 1982 by CIPFA Services Ltd., Granby Hunter and URBED. It is a unit trust aimed at attracting local authority pension funds to invest in property let to small businesses in their areas. At the same time it fills a funding gap by allowing those who develop small units to realise their investment. So far it has invested approximately £10 million, all in the London area.

Project references

PROJECT ADDRESS	Imperial Studios, Imperial Road, London SW10
CONTACT	London Small Business Property Trust, 3 Robert Street, London WC2N 6BH Telephone: 01–930 1255
PROJECT ARCHITECTS	ACB Design Consultancy
	Contact: Alain Bouvier, 318 Wandsworth Bridge Road, London SW6 2TZ.

5 Mantra House

Keighley, Bradford

1930's engineering works now re-used as small units. Local authority development using Urban Programme funding.

GOOD PRACTICES HIGHLIGHTED

- Selecting the Building

- Using Subcontractors

- Continuing Management

A local authority conversion of a redundant factory into small units which was motivated by the desire to combat local unemployment. The emphasis on high standards of finish and the absence of phasing contrasts with many private sector developments of this type, but an entrepreneurial approach has been introduced through the arrangements for managing the building.

Key Facts

Original Building	*Type:*	Factory
	Construction:	Brick and stone
	Date:	1930's plus 1870's wing
	Size:	50,000 sq.ft. (gross)
	Storeys:	2
	Location:	New town centre
	Configuration:	Square block + wing
	Condition:	Good
Concept	*New Use:*	Small units
	Developer:	Local authority
	Approach:	Local authority
	Manager:	Entrepreneurial service company
Finance	*Public Sector:*	£630,000
	Private Sector:	Nil
Development	*Tenure:*	Freehold
	Acquisition Cost:	£180,000
	Conversion Cost:	£450,000
	Date of Scheme:	1981–1983
	Lettable Area:	24,300 sq.ft.
	Cost per sq.ft. (gross):	£17.50 (1986 Equivalent: £22.00)*
	Cost per sq.ft. (net):	£26.00 (1986 Equivalent: £32.50)*
Result	*No. of Units:*	67 (Size Range 85 to 1350 sq.ft.)
	Employment:	150 approx.

*Adjusted for building cost inflation to approximate 1986 value

PROJECT SUMMARY

The building
Mantra Mills, a 50,000 sq.ft. engineering works, consisted of two 2-storey buildings joined together, a late Victorian mill and a large square block built in the 1930s. Both floors had industrial load bearing capacity and good natural light. The building was near the centre of Keighley and had only been empty for a month when the City of Bradford Metropolitan Council purchased it in 1981.

The problem
In the late 1970's and early 1980's, as the recession in manufacturing industry hit hard, many famous old firms which had been major employers in their localities went out of business. This was the case with Hattersleys of Keighley who were once one of the most famous textile engineering companies in the world. As a result local authorities like Bradford, although not traditionally involved in economic issues, found themselves in the front line in the fight to tackle local unemployment.

The scheme
In order to encourage more people to start their own businesses, Bradford's Economic Development Unit had decided to convert a large redundant building into small units. Mantra Mills seemed an ideal choice and, after demolishing much of the old wing to provide parking space, they converted the rest of the space into 67 units, using Urban Programme funding and the Council's own resources.

The outcome
The conversion work was successfully completed and Mantra House was opened in April 1983. There has been good demand for space. The management has been subcontracted to a local office services company which has taken a positive and energetic approach to helping the tenants.

Organisation and management of the project

INCUBATION STAGE

Objective
Administratively Keighley is part of the City of Bradford in the heart of what used to be Britain's textile industry. Because of the rapid decline of that industry Bradford Council had formed an Economic Development Unit whose task was to develop new jobs locally. The Mantra House scheme was initiated and organised by the Economic Development Unit. They had already received several requests for help and advice, especially about premises from Keighley people who were keen to start their own small businesses, but as the area had traditionally been dominated by large employers in large premises there was a shortage of small units. Their objective for the scheme, therefore, was to provide small units especially for start ups. They were not principally concerned with return on investment.

Organisation and approach
The Economic Development Unit organised the project, drawing on other Council departments as required. A surveyor in the Unit, Simon Woodhurst, played a leading role in the early stages but there does not appear to have been one main driving force. Later on, when Mantra House was in operation, a private firm, Link-Up Services Ltd., offered to run it and Margaret Elliot has become a remarkably positive manager, getting involved with the problems of the tenants' businesses, rather than just the problems of the building. Thus an entrepreneurial management stage was added on to what had been a fairly conventional local authority development. In this case, as financial return was not paramount, the transition caused no difficulty.

Selecting the building
In 1981 the Economic Development Unit were plann-

Figure 11: The derelict engineering works in 1981.

Figure 12: The basic units have good access and are spacious.

ing to provide small business units. After considering costs they had decided that new building would be too expensive and that conversion of an existing building ought to be much cheaper, if the right building could be found. They asked local estate agents to find buildings for them and within a week they heard of an engineering works in Keighley that had just come onto the market, it was Mantra Mills. Simon Woodhurst visited it with a Council architect, John Hurd, and was immediately certain that this building was right for conversion. It was in a good location. It was structurally sound, the only part in poor condition could be demolished to create a car park. There were load bearing floors, and the window placement would make subdivision easy. Only the roof needed major attention, though it would be difficult not to waste some of the internal space in the centre of the block (figure 11).

Obtaining the building on good terms

The City Council bought the building without delay. The previous owners had had to go into liquidation suddenly as a result of a court case. The freehold of the building was on their books at £250,000 and they wanted to sell it for as much as possible as quickly as possible. Simon Woodhurst negotiated them down to £180,000, about £3.50 per total sq.ft., but it is not clear whether this was a realistic market price. When Mantra House was fully converted it had only 24,300 sq.ft. of lettable space, which meant that the cost of the building was nearer £7.50 per sq.ft. on that basis.

Formulating the scheme

The outline of the scheme had been clear to Simon Woodhurst from the moment he first saw the building. Units could be made by building partition walls between each set of windows (figure 12). The detailed designs were done in early 1982 by a Council team consisting of Simon Woodhurst, John Hurd and two engineers. 67 units, varying in size from 100 sq.ft. to 1,250 sq.ft., were created along with reception, meeting room and canteen facilities. About two-thirds of the old mill wing was to be demolished to provide a car park, and a new main entrance was to be built. Conversion costs were estimated at £450,000. No detailed market analysis was required as the Economic Development Unit already knew of many firms and individuals seeking space.

In order to provide as much local employment as possible it was decided to use several local subcontractors working under a contractor employed on a management fee basis (See p. 54).

NEGOTIATION STAGE

Raising the finance

In Bradford's 1981–82 budget £250,000 had been provisionally allocated for building new small units. This project did not materialise and the budget was transferred to the purchase of Mantra House, and the money required for the conversion work was included in the 1982–83 budget. The scheme was eligible for support under the Urban Programme but was not initially among the high priority projects approved by the DoE. Bradford, however, pressed ahead with plans for the scheme and approached the DoE in the autumn of 1982 to see if any underspend funds were available. Additional resources were found and Urban Programme funding was approved in November 1982. A grant of £525,000 was authorised as a contribution to the total cost of the scheme. Bradford City Council met the remainder of the cost from its own resources.

Sources of finance

		£
Urban Programme (75% DoE)		394,000
	(25% Bradford)	131,000
Bradford City Council		105,000
		£630,000

Finding appropriate professionals

The Council had its own Development Services departments and was able to assemble its own professional team. Planning permission was not a problem, but fire regulations were quite onerous. The professional team were well able to handle the project.

Maintaining financial flexibility

Flexibility was not greatly emphasised in this project. The scheme was designed in detail in advance and the contract was let on a management fee basis. This meant that a professional project manager was brought in to ensure that the building works were carried out on time and within budget. This reduced the need for financial flexibility on the part of the Council.

Project management

Since the creation of local employment was uppermost in the Economic Development Unit's thinking, it was decided that, rather than employing one main contractor whose workforce would probably come from outside the area, the work should be split up among several local subcontractors who would work together under the direction of the project manager. This would ensure that local people were indeed working on the project. For this procedure to work it was necessary to have a reliable and experienced project manager who could work closely with the professional team, and so a major building firm, Laing's, were selected.

CONSTRUCTION STAGE

Using subcontractors

Laing's project manager, Malcolm Brumwell, handled the subcontractors very well and there was excellent co-operation on site. As many of those working on the building were local and realised the importance of the project to Keighley, there was much enthusiasm and determination to do the job well. There were thus no problems on the building side. As with many local authority schemes there was emphasis on a high standard of finish. For example the outside of the building was cleaned and the new gable wall by the car park was built in stone.

Keeping control of time and money

The management fee contract put responsibility for control of time and money into the hands of an experienced professional. There were no unexpected occurrences and the conversion was completed smoothly and on schedule.

MANAGEMENT STAGE

Marketing

The conversion work was carried out in one phase and was finished in March 1983. Marketing had already started some three months earlier. The Economic Development Unit already knew of many businesses which were interested in taking space and there was coverage of the scheme in the local press well before it opened. Simple monthly terms with a single all inclusive charge (to include rent, rates and basic management services) were arranged. A clear brochure was produced emphasising these 'easy-in, easy-out' terms and the services provided. The rents charged were not high (under £2 per sq.ft.) and would have given an expected initial yield of under 5% on the total investment (£630,000). However the Council had only invested £236,000 of its own resources in the scheme so that the expected yield to the Council, after allowing for voids, was over 12%, a perfectly satisfactory result.

As predicted, without the need for any sophisticated market research, there was good demand for space in Mantra House, and while there has been a comparatively high turn-over of tenants, as is only to be expected with a high proportion of business start-ups, average occupancy has remained high.

Continuing management

Originally the Economic Development Unit had intended to manage Mantra House itself, but one of the people who read about the scheme in the local press was Larry Gould, the Managing Director of Link-Up Services Ltd., an expanding office services company providing everything from translations to temporary staff, and he offered to manage the building. Not only could Link-Up offer a wide range of services but it had direct experience of managing premises and above all understood and sympathised with the needs of small firms. The Council was impressed with Link-Up and contracted out to them the management and marketing of Mantra House in return for a fee and a percentage of the rent.

Link-Up provided an excellent manager, Margaret Elliot, who not only had a breadth of experience in company administration, but also set out to create a positive atmosphere in the building. She has forged close links with the Local Enterprise Agency (see p. 54) which now holds a monthly surgery at Mantra House for the firms located there. Furthermore she takes a real interest in the firms and their problems. As well as managing the building she does all she can to promote their success. Thus a scheme which started out with a conventional local authority approach ended up with entrepreneurial management.

Notes

Management fee contract

A way of organising a building contract under which an outside project manager is brought in to supervise the contractors or subcontractors and ensure that they carry out the work as specified on time and within budget. The project manager takes a fee but relieves the developer, and his professional team, of direct responsibility for managing the building works.

Local Enterprise Agency

A local organisation which promotes new enterprise and local economic development in its area, usually sponsored by the local authority in partnership with major local firms, the Chamber of Commerce and banks. There are now approximately 250 Enterprise Agencies in Britain. **Business in the Community,** 227a City Road, London EC1 is a national organisation which promotes Local Enterprise Agencies.

Project references

PROJECT ADDRESS	Mantra House, South Street, Keighley, West Yorkshire Telephone: 0534–606233
CONTACT	Margaret Elliot
PROJECT ARCHITECTS	Directorate of Development Services, City of Bradford Metropolitan Council, Jacobs Well, Bradford BD1 5RW.

6 The Briggait

Clyde Street, Glasgow

Listed 19th and Early 20th Century fish market, now re-used as speciality shopping centre with food hall and food court. Developed in partnership by a charitable trust, and a leading financial institution, using public and private finance.

GOOD PRACTICES HIGHLIGHTED

- Forming a Trust
- Obtaining Public Support
- Raising the Finance
- Project Management

A triumph of goodwill and public and private sector collaboration over conventional property development wisdom. Enthusiastic conservationists formed a Trust and promoted a scheme to revive Glasgow's marvellous old fish market which caught the imagination of both the public and private sectors. Raising the finance and overcoming the obstacles of turning vision into reality took an enormous amount of personal effort and collaboration, but the scheme generated the goodwill to accomplish it.

Key Facts

Original Building	Type:	Market Halls
	Construction:	Iron and steel frames; glass roofs
	Date:	1873/1889/1904/1914
	Size:	43,000 sq.ft.
	Storeys:	One
	Location:	Edge of city centre
	Configuration:	Large empty spaces
	Condition:	Poor
Concept	New Use:	Speciality shopping centre
	Developer:	Conservation Trust + Institution
	Approach:	Conservationist
	Manager:	Professional retail manager
Finance	Public Sector:	£1.05 million
	Private Sector:	£1.45 million
Development	Tenure:	125-year lease
	Building Cost:	Nil
	Conversion Cost:	£2.5 million
	Date of Scheme:	1981–1986
	Lettable Area:	24,400 sq.ft.
	Cost per sq.ft. (gross):	£58 (1986 Equivalent: £60)*
	Cost per sq.ft. (net):	£103 (1986 Equivalent: £107)*
Result	No. of Units:	53 (plus 18 market stalls)
	Employment:	120

*Adjusted for building cost inflation to approximate 1986 value

Figure 13: The derelict exterior prior to renovation

Figure 14: The renovated arches house new business and shops

PROJECT SUMMARY

The building

The Briggait, once Glasgow's fishmarket, consists of three glass-roofed halls covering a one acre site on the north bank of the River Clyde near the city centre. Somewhat incongruously a 17th Century steeple is incorporated into the middle of it. The oldest hall (1873) is magnificent, with a high arched roof space and a gallery all around it. The internal cast iron work and the external facades are very fine.

The problem

The fishmarket moved out in 1977 and the buildings were left to deteriorate (figure 13). The site although central has been surrounded by dereliction for a long time, first due to the deterioration of inner Glasgow and more recently due to the massive redevelopment of nearby St. Enoch's Station. The river and a railway line also cut the site off on two sides. Permission to demolish the listed buildings was sought and refused. Local conservationsts decided in 1980 to try to save the Briggait.

The scheme

The scheme was to form a non-profit Trust to raise money from public and private sources and redevelop the Briggait through a subsidiary development company into a specialist shopping centre, with a cafe-theatre and small industrial and studio workspace. The professionals who had originated the scheme would be employed by the company to carry it through and profits from the development would be convenanted back to the Trust.

The outcome

The Bridgegate Trust was formed in 1982 and a joint-venture development company established. £1.5 million was successfully raised. Mid-way through the work it was realised that another £1.1 million was

required. When this was raised and professional project management brought in the scheme was completed and opened in April 1986. It is a splendid development and likely to become in time a major feature of Glasgow (Figure 14).

Organisation and management of the project

INCUBATION STAGE

Driving force

The driving force behind the Briggait project was the wish to save a very fine building. This idea was very attractive, but it is people not ideas that get things done. The two originators of the scheme were Jim Johnson an architect with an academic background, well-known in Glasgow for his innovative rehabilitation of tenement housing, and Tom Laurie an entrepreneurial quantity surveyor who was interested in setting up a Cafe-Theatre. These two were later

Figure 15: The high arched central hall and iron work restored to retail uses

joined by Douglas Hadfield, a former British Steel executive who shared their views.

Objective

The objective of the project was to save the decaying Fishmarket and bring it back into use, creating jobs and thereby helping to revitalise a run-down part of Glasgow. The scheme involved finding a new use for the buildings and raising the necessary finance, but no-one had a personal stake in the end use especially after Tom Laurie found another location for his Cafe-Theatre.

Formulating the scheme

Jim Johnson and Tom Laurie faced a daunting task. They were conservationists. They had no firm plans for the Fishmarket, no finance, no organisation, no direct development experience, no credibility and they did not own the buildings. In all property development ownership is crucial. Glasgow District Council owned the freehold. The first task therefore was to get ownership rights into the hands of a body that would be acceptable to the District Council, and acceptable to the conservationists so that their wishes would be carried out. Drawing on the experiences of David Rock and others, they proposed the formation of an independent non-profit Trust (see p. 59), controlled by sympathetic and respectable 'interested parties' and limited by guarantee, to take a long lease on the buildings. They spoke to as many interested parties as they could think of, including representatives of the local and regional councils. They put down their basic ideas on a free broadsheet and they called a public meeting, with a carefully invited guest list, at Strathclyde University in March 1981. This meeting endorsed the idea of a Trust and set up a Steering Committee which soon expanded to 14 members, plus 7 professional advisers (including Jim Johnson and Tom Laurie). George Dunlop, a leading Scottish businessman, was invited to become Chairman. The local authorities were not initially represented, but were later invited to appoint members of the Trust's Council.

Up to this time no-one had been paid. Indeed expenses had had to be met personally. The next step was to persuade the Scottish Development Agency (SDA) to give a grant to the professional team to carry out a feasibility study. In this case a fairly large grant of £14,000 was obtained, but the study had to include a detailed assessment of the condition of the structure and the costs of restoring it.

The feasibility study report, published in December 1981, was primarily technical. The costings related solely to construction costs. The financial analysis was limited to showing that the scheme would be viable when fully let if half the investment could be raised as grants. There was limited market assessment, and the details of how tenants would use the building had not been finalised. However the report showed that £400,000 would be required to make the buildings watertight and just over a further £1 million to convert them. Emphasis now switched to raising the money.

NEGOTIATION STAGE

Raising the finance

While the professionals were working on the feasibility study, Douglas Hadfield, began to look for money. For a whole year he was unpaid, but eventually the Trust obtained Urban Programme funding to cover its administrative costs. The Steering Committee proved a good sounding board but its members did not have the time nor the experience to take on active roles. Douglas Hadfield therefore did most of the fund raising work.

Glasgow District Council offered the buildings on a 125-year lease at a peppercorn rent (rising to 10% of net rental income after 5 years) and were prepared to give £250,000 towards the cost of refurbishment. This was a very substantial grant. Strathclyde Regional Council gave £100,000, and further grants were obtained from the Scottish Historic Buildings Council (£85,000) and the Scottish Tourist Board (£134,000 – although this was later withdrawn).

No private financial institution in Scotland could be persuaded to invest. However Prudential Assurance, one of the largest insurance companies in London, eventually agreed to invest £750,000. The Prudential's initial view of the project was not hopeful. To an experienced property investor's eye the Briggait site was a long way away from any established activity and on a wet winter's day it looked extremely bleak. However, as part of the Financial Institutions Group (see p. 59) the Prudential were keen to promote realistic inner city projects. It was clear that the Covent Garden market, opened in 1980, would be an outstanding success and the Briggait buildings were equally magnificent. After making some adjustments to the figures in the study, the Prudential could expect an initial return of 10% on their investment. Although they might normally have aimed for 20% on a risky scheme like this, 10% represented a reasonable average return for their property investments as a whole and they were prepared to accept it. They did not make their own detailed appraisal of the costings.

In mid 1982 there was still a funding gap of £181,000, but the SDA managed to arrange assistance through LEG-UP, the Scottish equivalent of Urban Development Grant. By enabling the Prudential's investment of £750,000 to go ahead this grant obtained leverage of over 4 to 1.

Thus, after two years of hard work the basic scheme had been devised, the interested parties brought together the £1.5 million required. Only the feasibility study money had been spent, all the rest was goodwill.

Legal structure

Sorting out the legal relationships took six more

months. The Bridgegate Trust was formally constituted as a company limited by guarantee with charitable status. It, in turn, formed a development company (a normal company, limited by shares) called The Briggait Company as a 50-50 joint venture with the Prudential. Each partner was investing £750,000 in the development company – the Trust's money coming entirely from public sector grants, the Prudential investing their own money. Each partner nominated three directors and had half-control of the company. Although George Dunlop, the Chairman of the Trust, became Chairman of the development company, the other two Trust directors were newcomers, one with building experience, the other to represent the interests of the public sector.

Once the development company had been set up, it and not the Trust became the real developer. The company, not the Trust, took the lease and was responsible for complying with its terms and with the various statutory requirements. The company, not the Trust, employed the professional team. The directors of the company, not the members of the Trust, felt personally responsible. The Trust had little direct influence during the development stage which caused resentment from time to time. A 50-50 joint venture is often a recipe for disaster in business and shareholders' agreements were drawn up in case deadlock occurred, but in the event all the directors were so committed to completing the development that there was no rift.

Maintaining financial flexibility

Although the Prudential owned 50% of the share capital of the development company, they wished for tax reasons to take their money out as interest payments, not dividends. However, the Prudential did not wish to burden the project with a normal fixed interest loan, which would have put it under severe financial strain in its early years. They therefore arranged their investment as a secured loan whose interest rate varied according to the company's income. Thus the Prudential would receive their return in the form of interest, the amount of which would be governed by the success of the project. The Trust would receive an equal sum of money covenanted to it by the company, and the rent payable to the District Council after the five rent-free years would also be directly related to rental income. In this way, once the development was complete, the company's main costs would be related to its income, giving it great financial flexibility. However as far as the conversion costs were concerned there was no flexibility. £1.5 million was the limit of the company's funds.

CONSTRUCTION STAGE

Using contractors

Phase 1 of the building works was to make the buildings watertight. While consideration had originally been given to using an MSC workforce it had been decided that the specialised work required made this impractical. Furthermore the work had to be done without delay as the deterioration was continuing. Quotations were sought from several contractors and the lowest was chosen. Work began at the end of 1982, but the roof work caused more problems than anticipated and involved substantial extra costs. The lowest quotation is not always the best value.

Project management

The same highly committed professional team, led by Jim Johnson, that had been behind the scheme from its inception had been employed to design and implement the scheme. While Phase 1 went ahead, detailed designs were prepared for Phase 2, the conversion and fitting out of the speciality shopping centre and workshop and studio units. It soon became apparent that the original costings made when the scheme was still only a vision had been optimistic. The full details of how the tenants and the public would use the buildings had not been previously worked out, nor had project management or marketing been adequately allowed for.

Faced with an alarming rise in costs, and no funds to cover it, the directors invited Richard Ellis, well known surveyors and estate agents, to re-examine the concept and to provide experienced project management. Richard Ellis advised raising the scheme's specification and making it more up-market. They suggested including a Food Court and heating for the buildings, all of which increased costs still further. The Prudential had not yet made any investment and could have pulled out. The potential for conflict between the professional team and Richard Ellis, and between the unpaid directors and the professionals, was immense. There was some ill-feeling but it was overcome by the over-riding determination of all parties to see the project continue and succeed, and after a year's delay a reduced version of the new scheme was agreed. Although lettable space was decreased from 48,000 sq.ft. to 24,400 sq.ft. the total estimated cost rose from £1.5 million to over £2.5 million (£100 per sq.ft. of lettable space)

These were anxious times while the extra money was raised. The SDA arranged a further £400,000 through LEG-UP and the Prudential invested another £700,000 in return for the right to receive 84% of the rental income. Even so the Prudential's estimated return fell from 10% to 7% and the return to the Trust virtually disappeared. Once more, however, goodwill enabled the necessary compromises to be made.

Sources of finance	£
Prudential Assurance	1,450,000
Scottish Development Agency	581,000
Glasgow District Council	250,000
Scottish Historic Buildings Council	110,000
Strathclyde Regional Council	100,000
Bridgegate Trust	20,000
	£2,511,000

Just when the revised Phase 2 was about to start in early 1984, VAT was introduced on building alterations. Eventually listed buildings were zero rated, but the directors could not wait for this point to be settled and they decided to let and pay for the entire contract in advance. Highly reliable contractors had to be chosen, therefore, and this proved an advantage. The second phase proceeded smoothly, on time and on budget, a tribute to Ian Burnett the project manager.

MANAGEMENT STAGE

Marketing

The Briggait was finally opened in April 1986, nearly six years after the project started. The site is still isolated, and will continue to be so until the development of St. Enoch's is complete. Nevertheless the new Briggait is visually exciting and a series of events have been planned to attract people in. The local press has been very positive. Marketing is in the hands of a local estate agent and the scheme has been widely advertised. There are 53 retail and restaurant units (figure 15), and 18 market stalls which are let on a daily or weekly basis. There is a full time Centre Manager based on the site. There is room for entertainments and other events in the main hall. Over half of the units were let within a few weeks of the opening, many to new businesses, and care was taken to choose tenants with special products to sell. The Food Court, however, still needs to be made to work. Nevertheless there is confidence that in time the Briggait will be a huge success.

Notes

Trust. A body which is responsible for managing money given to it for a specified purpose. It is often used in the name of organisations to imply that their aim is public, rather than private, benefit. A Trust undertaking property development is often constituted as a **Company Limited by Guarantee,** which has no shareholders and may not distribute profits, yet the individuals running it are not personally liable for its debts if things go wrong.

Financial Institutions Group (FIG): A group of 26 leading financial institutions which were invited by the Secretary of State for the Environment to send a representative to visit Liverpool with him in the Summer of 1981 to learn about inner city problems. During the next year they put forward ideas and initiatives to help promote urban regeneration.

Project references

PROJECT ADDRESS	The Briggait, 72 Clyde Street, Glasgow G1 2LO Telephone: 041 552–3970
CONTACT	Hugh O'Donnell, Centre Manager
PROJECT ARCHITECTS	ASSIST Architects, 6 Dixon Street, Glasgow G1 4AX

7 Waterfront Hotel

Dagger Lane, Hull

19th Century listed warehouses, now re-used as nightclub, hotel and restaurant. Individual developer using direct labour. Mostly privately financed.

GOOD PRACTICES HIGHLIGHTED

- Driving Force
- Entrepreneurial Approach
- Formulating the Scheme
- Obtaining Public Support
- Maintaining Flexibility
- Using Your Own Workforce
- Keeping Control of Time and Money
- Continuing Management

An extreme example of the entrepreneurial approach. An individual with a scheme which was so far-fetched that it was laughed out of court initially, turned it into reality single handedly through 'do-it-yourself', cutting corners and the use of internal cash flow to finance successive stages.

Key Facts

Original Building	*Type:*	Warehouses
	Construction:	Brick
	Date:	1831/1870
	Size:	36,000 sq.ft.
	Storeys:	4 (plus basement)
	Location:	Centre of Old Town
	Configuration:	3 narrow buildings
	Condition:	Derelict
Concept	*New Use:*	Hotel/Night Club
	Developer:	Individual
	Approach:	Entrepreneurial
	Manager:	Original developer
Finance	*Public Sector:*	£49,500
	Private Sector:	£98,500
Development	*Tenure:*	99-year lease
	Acquisition Cost:	Nil
	Conversion Cost:	£148,000
	Date of Scheme:	1977
	Useable Area:	32,000 sq.ft.
	Cost per sq.ft. (gross):	£4.10 (1986 Equivalent: £6.50)*
	Cost per sq.ft. (net):	£4.60 (1986 Equivalent: £7.50)*
Result	*No. of Units:*	32 rooms (plus club, restaurants)
	Employment:	90 (including part-time)

*Adjusted for building cost inflation to approximate 1986 value

PROJECT DESCRIPTION

The building
The Waterfront Hotel and Club were created out of three derelict dockside warehouses, the oldest of which (Grade II listed), dated back to 1831. All three were soldily built in red brick with timber beams and floors and were located in the centre of Hull's Old Town, an area with twisting lanes and many fine buildings but which had become very run down.

The problem
By 1977 the warehouses had been empty for nearly 20 years. Their roofs had given way with a tree growing out at one point. They were surrounded by decay and the City Council was planning comprehensive redevelopment. However Francis Daly decided that this would be a splendid place to live, so long as he could develop a scheme with a rapid pay back, which would enable him to build himself a penthouse flat.

The scheme
Francis Daly decided to convert the first warehouse into a licensed club, aimed particularly at young professional people. He undertook the building work himself and deliberately retained as much as possible of the old building and its fixtures. In six months the club was open and highly successful. In order to make full use of the catering and other services already in the club he started converting the other buildings into hotel rooms. As more money became available so he built more rooms.

The Outcome
The Waterfront Hotel now has 32 rooms, and it, too, is highly successful. New life is returning to the Old Town. People now live there once more and many buildings are being repaired or converted.

Organisation and management of the project

INCUBATION STAGE

Driving force
The Waterfront project was very much the creation of one person, Francis Daly. Not only did he initiate and mastermind the project, but he also carried out much of the work himself from the beginning to the end of the scheme. For several years his entire life revolved around the Waterfront project.

Francis Daly has energy, enthusiasm and charm. He likes doing things and he likes getting things done. He likes to do things his way and he can be very tactless. He also works very hard. He does not claim to have any special talents except persistence and a dislike of pomposity. Like so many people he has good ideas, and like so few he puts them into practice – in a sensible, straight forward way.

Objectives
The main reason that Francis Daly became involved in Waterfront was that he wanted somewhere to live. He was attracted by the dereliction of Hull's Old Town because it reminded him of his native Ireland, but he also saw it as a place of great charm with narrow streets, disused docks and fine buildings, and close enough to the city centre to be brought back to life. He had already dabbled in property, while at university, renovating houses and letting out rooms to fellow students. However changes in the Rent Act made residential property unattractive. By 1977 he was looking for a scheme which would generate sufficient cash for him to live off and enable him to build a flat of his own. He also wanted to do something which would bring activity back into the neighbourhood. He hit on the idea of a night club because it was the sort of place which he would like to go to himself and which did not exist in Hull at the time. It would bring activity back to the Old Town and could be very profitable.

Figure 16: The roof was not completely watertight

62

Figure 17: The scene before work was begun

'I had this picture in my mind of people sipping coffee and liqueurs, like I had seen them on the Continent.'

Selecting the buildings

Francis Daly wanted a waterfront building. The warehouses on the corner of Dagger Lane attracted him. They looked out across Prince's Dock and were not too far from economically active parts of the City. However the buildings had been empty for 18 years and were very delapidated (figures 16 and 17). The lead had been stripped from the roofs which had partially collapsed, but Francis Daly satisfied himself that, whatever a professional surveyor might advise, the structures were basically sound.

Formulating the scheme

With these particular buildings in mind, Francis Daly began thinking of how to develop his scheme while making as few changes as possible. The basic idea was for the listed warehouse to become a club and for the others to be converted into flats, as money became available from the profits of the club. The building itself with its beams, its views, and its nooks and crannies would provide most of the night club atmosphere. Partial demolition of the roof would save rebuilding it all and provide materials for the rest. With his engineering degree, with some past building experience, and with a strong feel for the type of place he wished to create, Francis Daly set about working out a detailed scheme for his club. It was not a question of doing a feasibility study, but of thinking through each problem and each opportunity so as to produce a good solution at the lowest cost.

> 'These things takes a lot of thinking about. You cannot just design and cost up a conversion scheme like a new office block – or if you do it will cost you the earth. I am often awake at four in the morning thinking about some little details and I'll often make some notes or a sketch there and then . . . If I think about problems enough, I know I will eventually find the answer . . . It's like that all the way through, as the building work goes on, so you find you can adapt and change things and make them better.'

The first phase of the scheme was to be the club. It was only later that he realised that the facilities provided by the club make it sensible to convert the rest of the property into a hotel rather than flats. But with one person in sole change, it was not difficult to modify.

NEGOTIATION STAGE

Obtaining the building on good terms

Like most of the rest of the Old Town the buildings were owned by the City Council who were hoping to carry out a comprehensive redevelopment scheme at some time in the future. They intially offered a 5-year lease. But the Industrial Development Department was in favour of rehabilitation schemes so long as they were commercially sound and supported the Waterfront project. Eventually in early 1978 a 99-year lease, with an intitial rent holiday during the construction period, was granted, provided that a liquor licence could be obtained.

Obtaining public support

Francis Daly discussed his proposals with the police and the fire brigade. Armed with the plans he had drawn up himself, he applied for his licence and was literally laughed out of court. For his second application he felt that he needed professional legal advice, but so great had been the previous fiasco that nobody in Hull would take on his case and he had to find help outside. Even so he lost again because he failed to prove that there really was a demand for another place serving alcohol. Before his third application, therefore, he held an Open Day, courted the Civic Society and other local interest bodies, drew up subscription lists and obtained coverage in the local newspaper. On the day itself he packed the court with his supporters. He received his provisional licence, and consequently his lease.

Raising the finance

Francis Daly wanted to do things his own way, organising the building work himself rather than using building professionals and contractors. He was certain that this would save a lot of money, but realised that he would have to finance the project himself. He had hoped to obtain finance from one of the brewery companies in return for selling their products, but they all continued to oppose his scheme as it might jeopardize their existing Old Town customers. The total cost of the first phase was £65,000. The City Council gave a grant of £1,500 and the Historic Buildings Commission gave £5,000. All the rest came from personal sources.

For the second phase, converting the other buildings into a Hotel, the picture was very different. First money flowed in from the profits of the club. The Yorkshire and Humberside Tourist Board provided a grant of £35,000. Further grants came from the Historic Buildings Commission and from Humberside County Council. And, once the success of the club had been established, several breweries became interested in providing finance and a £40,000 loan was arranged. The Waterfront now sells more beer than any other outlet in Hull.

Sources of finance

	£
Personal Resources and Reinvestment	58,500
Brewery Loan	40,000
Yorkshire and Humberside Tourist Board	35,000
Historic Buildings Commission	12,000
Hull City Counil	1,500
Humberside County Council	1,000
	£148,000

Maintaining flexibility

Flexibility has been one of Francis Daly's basic principles. By keeping everything under his own direct control and minimising the involvement of outsiders he has been able to modify things as he goes along so as to take advantage of opportunities as they arise, to get things done faster and to keep the work in line with the availability of cash.

His approach was highly entrepreneurial. Not only did he take a phased approach, starting first with the club, then developing the hotel and adding more rooms in stages, he also obtained many materials second hand and often very cheaply – for example some of the seats were pews from a disused church. Furthermore, if things did not feel quite right, walls were moved and features redesigned during the course of the building work, so as to achieve the best results at the lowest cost.

Finding appropriate professionals

Basically Francis Daly did without professionals. He knew what he wanted and he found it better to do things himself rather than through others. He drew up all the plans for both the club and hotel himself, using as guidelines, for example, the AA and RAC hotel inspectors' evaluation criteria. He preferred to deal directly with the planning, building and fire authorities as matters which could have huge financial implications were often at stake. He only used an architect to draw up the final version of his plans.

> 'It would have been impossible for me to describe to a professional architect exactly what I was seeking to produce. It would also have made it impossible for me to keep on altering and redesigning small details as the project took shape.'

CONSTRUCTION STAGE

Using your own workforce

On nearly all conversion projects the driving force is content to leave the actual building work to others, but this was not the case with Francis Daly. Just as people find that they can save a great deal of money through 'do-it-yourself' in their own homes so he was convinced that doing his own conversion work himself would be very much cheaper. He therefore formed his own building firm, Conservation and Construction Ltd., (or Con and Con), starting with one man and ending up with fourteen. Not many developers have the experience to undertake serious building work and funding institutions are not likely to favour this approach either, but nevertheless Francis Daly carried out a sizeable scheme himself, and is convinced that he could not possibly have afforded to do it any other way.

With the boss working directly as foreman, the work went very quickly. It took only six months from start to finish to carry out the first phase and open the club. The Con and Con philosophy was to make the least change possible to the buildings. They were fine old buildings. What was required was to work round what already existed, making features out of the original structures and fittings, even if they were not perfect. The same principles were also applied to the hotel which was developed when funds became available from the club. First 13 rooms were built to ensure that there was suffient demand. The rooms were simple, almost spartan, but with interesting shapes, bare brickwork and beams, and very different from most modern hotels. The public areas were spacious and interesting, making use again of the character of the buildings. Gradually new rooms were added making a total of 32.

Keeping control of time and money

Francis Daly controlled everything by being personally involved. He controlled the money by holding the purse strings. He also clearly saw that time was money. Not only did delays cost money, they also put off the day when income would be received. He used no sophisticated control charts but believed in the value of deadlines in the building industry where small pieces of work can drag on and on preventing a job from being finished. He therefore set tough deadlines, such as an official opening day, which forced everything to be ready – if not absolutely finished – by a specific date. These deadlines became challenges to which the whole team responded, and the work was done extremely quickly.

MANAGEMENT STAGE

Marketing

Nightclubs and hotels need customers, and continuous effort and energy have to be put into attracting them. The club got off to a flying start because of all the publicity surrounding the licence application. But frequent events are still held to keep up interest among the members. Also every 2 or 3 years there has been a deliberate effort to change the atmosphere in at least one part of the club. However, as there is now a waiting list to join the club, most of the marketing is aimed at ensuring that people enjoy the club when they use it and so use it more often. Francis Daly and his management partner, Angela Wilson, both spend a lot of time at the club.

For the hotel there was a grand opening with local dignitaries and businessmen invited. Promotional activity has been largely restricted to the Yorkshire and Humberside areas, and the local tourist board has featured the Waterfront in several of its campaigns. Particular efforts have been focussed on local businesses, and during the week the hotel is nearly always full. It has an interesting atmosphere, cheerful and efficient staff and reasonable prices.

Continuing management

Francis Daly did not just create the Waterfront, he lived on the site and with Angela Wilson actively managed it. This was crucial. He had created a place which he thought would attract people, but the building was only a means to an end, someone still had to keep putting in the energy to bring the place alive and make it go on attracting people day after day. Since the club was the type of club he had always wanted to go to himself it was not too painful to spend time there. But spending time there was important and so was making sure that the customers enjoyed themselves. As with the hotel, a great deal of emphasis was put on staff training and on team spirit and the results are immediately obvious.

It is only now, eight years after the start of the project, that a full time manager is being brought in. The hotel and club are well established successes. The Old Town has begun to revive and Francis Daly is turning his attention elsewhere.

Project references

PROJECT ADDRESS	Waterfront Hotel and Club, Dagger Lane, Old Town, Kingston upon Hull, HU1 2LS. Telephone: 0482–227222
CONTACT	Francis Daly
PROJECT ARCHITECTS	None

8 Watershed

Canons Road, Bristol

Two 19th Century dockside warehouses, now re-used as media centre, radio station and shopping arcade. Developed by established property development company using public and private finance, including commercial sponsorship.

GOOD PRACTICES HIGHLIGHTED

- Driving force
- Formulating the Scheme
- Raising the Finance
- Attracting Sponsorship
- Maintaining Financial Flexibility
- Project Management

An unconventional development by conventional developers, who deliberately supported and underwrote their principal client, to enable it to concentrate on setting up a vigorous and self-sustaining media centre. During the course of the project the role of driving force was successfully transferred from those who conceived the scheme initially to those who had to make the media centre work. The developers provided great financial flexibility which was crucial to the success of a risky, innovative project. In contrast the more conventional shopping side of the project had not yet been so successful.

Key Facts

Original Building	Type:	Warehouses
	Construction:	Brick
	Date:	1894
	Size:	47,000 sq.ft.
	Storeys:	2
	Location:	On quay, at edge of city centre
	Configuration:	Two narrow buildings
	Condition:	Partly sound, partly poor
Concept	New Use:	Media centre/ shopping
	Developer:	Development company
	Approach:	Entrepreneurial
	Manager:	Media centre + Developer
Finance	Public Sector:	£206,000
	Private Sector:	£1,549,500
Development	Tenure:	99-year lease
	Acquisition Cost:	Nil
	Conversion Cost:	£1.75 million
	Date of Scheme:	1979–1982
	Useable Area:	42,000 sq.ft.
	Cost per sq.ft. (gross):	£37.20 (1986 Equivalent: £49.50)*
	Cost per sq.ft. (net):	£41.50 (1986 Equivalent: £55.00)*
Result	No. of Units:	Not relevant
	Employment:	50

*Adjusted for building cost inflation to approximate 1986 value

Figure 18: The roof was virtually non-existant

PROJECT SUMMARY

The building

Watershed is made up of two 2 storey Victorian warehouses which run along the quayside of Bristol's Floating Harbour. They are listed buildings and in a Conservation Area just on the edge of the city centre. Other buildings around the quay have been renovated, but behind Watershed there is a large area of derelict goods yards.

The problem

After the Floating Harbour closed, Bristol City Council wished to bring the area back to life. They were planning large scale redevelopment of the goods yards, but wanted a mixed public-and-commercial use for the Watershed buildings. JT, a Bristol based developer, knew that the Bristol Arts Centre were seeking to expand and by incorporating them into its proposals obtained a 99-year lease from the City Council in 1979.

Figure 19: The dockside arcade required completion

The scheme

The scheme involved JT converting the ground floors into a speciality shopping arcade, which would be well positioned in relation to the goods yard development, and the upper floors into performance and exhibition areas for the Arts Centre. It also involved developing their major tenant from a modest community group into an organisation capable of equipping, financing and managing a major new arts centre. To do this JT found and supported a project director for the newly created Watershed Arts Trust.

The outcome

The Council cancelled the goods yard redevelopment. There was a palace revolution at the Arts Centre. But the conversion work went ahead on schedule and Watershed opened in 1982. The arts centre, now a 'media centre', focussing on film, video and photography, draws in 500,000 customers a year and has succeeded beyond expectation. However the shopping, which was intended to underpin the whole development commercially, has not yet been able to reach its full potential.

The organisation and management of the project

INCUBATION STAGE

Driving force

JT was the initial driving force behind the Watershed project. JT is a medium sized property development and construction group, operating throughout Britain and overseas. It has its own design, construction and property management capabilities. Its headquarters are in Bristol in a fine dockside building which it restored itself, and which also houses the Arnolfini Arts Centre. From there Watershed is clearly visible across the water. JT is fully commercial, but its Chairman and its Managing Director, John Pontin and Roger Mortimer, are interested in the arts and in

Figure 20: The well appointed restaurant and cafe

Bristol, and they were attracted to the idea of a mixed arts-and-commercial development for the Watershed buildings. Furthermore, if JT made a good job of Watershed its chances of being selected to develop the much larger goods yard next door might be increased.

Objective

As far as JT was concerned Watershed was primarily a commercial scheme. Not only were there to be 15,000 sq.ft. of retail space but 9,000 sq.ft. of offices and studios for the local radio station, Radio West, were also incorporated. JT did not think that they would achieve a normal developers return of 20% on this project, because they recognised that 15,000 sq.ft. of shopping space on its own was too small and would be expensive to manage, but nevertheless, given time, the commercial side of the development would pay off

The arts centre, however, was risky. But the directors of JT wanted to see it succeed and felt they could bend the rules a little to make this happen. The risks were two-fold. First, the Arts Trust might not be able to raise all the money to pay for the conversion and fitting out of its space. This would cause difficulties for JT who, as developers, were to all intents and purposes underwriting this part of the scheme. The second risk was that the Arts Trust, even if it succeeded in raising all the initial capital, might not be able to cover its running costs and would eventually go out of business. Only if the Arts Trust raised all the money required and then operated its new facilities successfully would JT avoid trouble. In fact JT had nothing to gain financially from the arts centre part of the development – except that it was the key to obtaining the lease for the project as a whole – but stood to lose substantially if it failed.

Formulating the scheme

JT had a well established 'design and build' capability (see p. 112). The in-house team was able to design and cost the scheme quite easily. The buildings were in a mixed condition. Bristol City Council had recently spent £115,000, financed by the Historic Buildings Commission, on one of the buildings. But, the roof of the other building needed replacing (figure 18), the dockside arcade needed completing (figure 19) and the two buildings had to be linked together. Then extensive internal fitting out had to be done, both for arts centre and for the shops. The total cost would be £1.6 million, of which £750,000 would have to come from the newly formed Watershed Arts Trust (even though JT agreed to charge preferential building rates on this work).

The crucial part of the scheme, therefore, was not the organising of the building work, but the organising of the Watershed Arts Trust to ensure that it could carry out its role. As a condition of being granted its 99-year lease JT had had to agree to lease most of the first floor to the Arts Trust for a peppercorn rent. The Bristol Arts Centre, out of which the new Arts Trust grew, had been principally a community theatre

centre, with a secondary interest in film, but by the end of the 1970's community theatre was beginning to suffer a decline, especially as local authority finances were cut back. JT therefore thought it wise to see that the Arts Trust was strengthened by someone with a proven track record in fund raising and through the Dartington Bristol Trust they arranged for Tony Byrne from the Ironbridge Gorge Museum to become full-time Project Director for the Arts Trust. JT also arranged for Dartington to take on a substantial part of the retail space.

JT did not do a detailed feasibility study. Nor did it feel the need to. There were no risk financiers to convince. The Arts Trust would not be paying rent, and the rents available from the shops and the radio station were known approximately. As with many commercial developers, the 'feasibility study' boiled down to a single sheet of financial calculations – anything more elaborate would only be produced, where necessary, as an external selling document.

NEGOTIATION STAGE

Obtaining the building on good terms

The freeholders, Bristol City Council, had offered a 99-year lease for a mixed public-commercial use in return for a half share in the rental income. Other schemes were submitted in competition with JT's, some offering a higher return to the Council, but no other scheme incorporated such truly public uses as the Watershed Arts Trust and Radio West, and so in the end JT's scheme was accepted.

Raising the finance

JT was a well established development company. It therefore had no difficulty in raising money from its own resources and from its bankers. The real challenge was for the Watershed Arts Trust to raise its share of the finance, to cover not only the initial capital costs, but also any deficit on running costs. One of the main reasons JT brought in Tony Byrne was to raise funds on behalf of the Arts Trust, for it soon became clear that community theatre would receive little backing and the previous manager resigned.

Fortunately Tony and Steve Pinhay, who took over as Artistic Director of Watershed and later became its first Chief Executive, developed the same vision of the arts centre in action and worked together towards that goal. This was fortuitous as neither had been involved in developing the original scheme, but by the time the building work went ahead, Tony and Steve had taken on the role of driving force for the arts centre side and were working together to produce an exciting Watershed which both customers and sponsors would find attractive. Their minds were very much fixed on the successful end-use of the building as a 'media centre', based on film, video and photography. While JT continued to provide an invaluable umbrella, particularly on the financial side, Tony and Steve took over the crucial role of pushing the 'media arts centre' side of the scheme through. And Steve stayed on to run it when it was completed.

Their first task was to raise money, and this they had to do by selling their concept of Britain's first 'media centre' to potential sponsors. Public funding for the arts was extremely tight. Local authority finance was coming under increasing pressure and was not likely to provide funds on the scale required. The arts were not a high priority area for the Urban Programme, nor was Bristol then a priority location. Commercial spnsorship, therefore, became the keystone of the financing strategy.

Attracting sponsorship

Attracting large-scale commercial sponsorship is still considered as something of an unknown art, although it is becoming increasingly common in sport and in the arts. But at bottom it is just another form of marketing, which depends on convincing each potential sponsor that they will benefit by being associated with the success of some new project. Confidence building and an understanding of the sponsor's objectives are the essential parts of it and these require a determined and professional approach.

The strategy for Watershed was to gain the support of at least one major national art-funding institution (to endorse the project's credibility) and then to involve as many Bristol based companies as possible. The general message was that something unique, something exciting, something of national standing was about to be launched in Bristol. The exact meaning of the term 'media and communications centre' may not have been clear, but the idea of a speciality film centre with a stream of imaginative events was well conveyed and appealing. The process of obtaining sponsors was arduous. Approaches were made to all major firms and institutions which had Bristol or film connections. Dozens of presentations were made and followed up. The one common factor was the need to find an individual who had both the authority to commit funds, and a personal interest in supporting the scheme.

> 'There is nothing magic about getting sponsorship. It is slow hard work, building brick by brick. You have to be patient and sympathetic to the wishes of the companies and the individuals in them, and above all you must show that you can deliver success. You are selling an opportunity'

In setting their standards Tony Byrne and Steve Pinhay decided that they would aim for an environment which distinguished foreign visitors would feel comfortable in. If it was attractive to them, it would also be attractive to the people of Bristol. Higher, and more expensive standards of finish were specified; facilities for the disabled and the hard of hearing were provided. All this added to the amount of sponsorship required. It was a difficult balance to make, but commercial sponsors wish to be proud of the schemes

that they support, and so while the emphasis at Watershed is on function not luxury, standards are deliberately high (figure 20).

The key sponsor was the British Film Institute which provided initial grants of £126,000 and has continued to support the project with substantial annual grants, second only to those it gives to the National Film Theatre in London. London Life Association provided a £220,000 loan at low interest rates. Sun Life Assurance gave £25,000. British Telecom paid for an advanced wiring and communications system and numerous other firms sponsored specific equipment and materials, or contributed towards the cost of events at Watershed. The Bristol Arts Centre invested £98,500 from the sale of its previous building. The Historic Buildings Commission made a £30,000 grant and Bristol City Council, as well as charging no rent for the area occupied by the arts centre, made a grant of £50,000.

Maintaining financial flexibility

JT in conjunction with the Dartington Bristol Trust played a crucial role. Not only was JT the developer and builder, but it also acted as banker and enabled the project to move ahead before all the financial sponsorship had been arranged. Furthermore, grants and allowances on building costs totalling some £140,000 were made. In addition up to £150,000 of low cost finance has been made available, some of which is still outstanding four years after the building work has been completed.

Thus, even though over £1 million has now been collected in sponsorship and the arts centre is a bustling success, the fact that JT was willing to act as banker and underwriter made a vital contribution. Without it, it is very unlikely that the scheme could have gone ahead. Where funding has to be raised from many different sources the importance of having some mechanism for maintaining financial flexibility cannot be over-emphasised.

Sources of finance

	£
London Life Assurance Loan	220,000
British Film Institute Grant	126,000
Bristol Arts Centre Donation	98,500
Bristol City Council Grant	50,000
Historic Buildings Commission Grant	30,000
Sun Life Assurance Grant	25,000
Charitable Trusts Grants	16,000
JT – Grants and Allowances	140,000
– Bridging Loan	150,000
Commercial Finance for Watershed Shopping	900,000
	£1,755,500*

*In addition, equipment, materials and services were donated by a range of commercial sponsors, which reduced the total project cost.

CONSTRUCTION STAGE

Project management

JT had its own experienced 'design and build' subsidiary, JT Design Build, which carried out all aspects of the conversion work, just as it would have done for a normal client. The project architect was Robert Trapnell and the project manager was Peter Bray. The construction work was completed on schedule and to a high standard.

The remarkable feature of this scheme was the creation of the Arts Trust project management, which enabled a new concept for the arts centre, with its own driving force, to emerge. Thus the baton was successfully passed from the original initiators (JT) to the person dedicated to the continuing success of the arts centre (Steven Pinhay), via a professional intermediary (Tony Byrne). Good fortune may have played an important part, because neither of the two subsequently crucial individuals was identified at the start. Alternatively it may just be that there are many people around who are capable of making a success of innovative projects so long as the right framework can be provided. JT certainly provided that framework.

MANAGEMENT STAGE

Watershed opened in 1982. The arts centre has two cinemas, film, video and photographic workshop space, studios, an exhibition space and a restaurant – all in 24,000 sq.ft. It has a lively film programme interspersed with major events and festivals. The bulk of its revenue comes from its paying customers, and with the continuing sponsorship of the British Film Institute and others it is now self-sufficient and an important part of Bristol's cultural scene. Marketing continues to be crucial. First, the paying customers have to be attracted in, mostly by the film programme which is widely publicised locally and through events which are heavily promoted through brochures, press and other media coverage and advertising. At the same time it is necessary to keep sponsorship money flowing in, which requires more direct personal contact. The lessons learned during the initial fund raising apply in just the same way.

Continuing management

The media centre draws in 500,000 customers a year and running the centre efficiently is one of Steve Pinhay's chief responsibilities. The shopping arcade on the ground floor is managed more traditionally by JT's own Management Department and the shops are let out to speciality retailers. But it is the media centre which is the real success story of the Watershed project and it has already become an important part of Bristol's cultural scene.

Project references

PROJECT ADDRESS	Watershed, 1 Canon's Road, Bristol BS1 5TX
	Telephone: 0272–276444
CONTACT	Steve Pinhay, Director
PROJECT ARCHITECTS	JT Design Build, 72 Prince Street, Bristol BS1 4HU.

9 Granby House

Granby Row, Manchester

[handwritten: Barn Conversion, Broadmore, Nottinghamshire]

Listed Edwardian cotton warehouse, now re-used as 61 flats. Developed by a housing association using private and public finance including Urban Development Grant.

GOOD PRACTICES HIGHLIGHTED

- Driving force
- Conventional Approach
- Selecting the Building
- Formulating the Scheme
- Selecting a Reliable Contractor

While the conversion of warehouse into flats is common practice in London because of the high price of housing, an element of subsidy is still required in other cities where flats sell for very much less. This example illustrates how the conventional approach to property development can be applied to conversion schemes where the product can be sold as a conventional investment. It also shows how Urban Development Grant may be used to make conventional development feasible for appropriate schemes which require an element of subsidy.

Key Facts

Original Building	Type:	~~Warehouse~~ *[handwritten: Barns & Stables]*
	Construction:	Brick
	Date:	~~1908~~ *[handwritten: 1807]*
	Size:	70,000 sq.ft. (gross)
	Storeys:	~~6 (plus basement)~~ *[handwritten: 1 + hay loft]*
	Location:	Near city centre *[handwritten: Broadmore]*
	Configuration:	Tall and square *[handwritten: low & square]*
	Condition:	~~Good~~ *[handwritten: Poor → Good]*
Concept	New Use:	~~Flats~~ *[handwritten: Housing]*
	Developer:	~~Housing Association~~ *[handwritten: K. & Holdings]*
	Approach:	Conventional
	Manager:	Sold to owner occupiers
Finance	Public Sector:	~~£575,000~~
	Private Sector:	~~£1,115,000~~
Development	Tenure:	Freehold
	Acquisition Cost:	~~£210,000~~ *[handwritten: 16,000]*
	Conversion Cost:	~~£1,480,000~~ *[handwritten: 30,000]*
	Date of Scheme:	~~1983–1985~~ *[handwritten: 1997]*
	Lettable Area:	~~56,000 sq.ft.~~
	Cost per sq.ft. (gross):	~~£24.10 (1986 Equivalent: £26.00)*~~
	Cost per sq.ft. (net):	~~£30.20 (1986 Equivalent: £32.50)*~~
Result	No. of Units:	~~61 flats~~ *[handwritten: Bar]*
	Employment:	Not relevant

*Adjusted for building cost inflation to approximate 1986 value

PROJECT SUMMARY

The building
Granby House is a fine 6 storey red brick building, with an interesting facade. It was built in 1908 as a cotton warehouse. It is Grade II listed and in a Conservation Area which contains many fine, and mostly empty, industrial buildings. Although largely unused it was in 1983 still in good structural order.

The problem
Granby House is in the heart of Manchester, but for many years people and industry have been moving out. As with many cities this had led to a lifeless core. What was needed was to encourage young people to live in the centre again. But how could this be done without prohibitive expense?

The scheme
The conversion of an existing building into an attractive block of flats ought to provide the solution, so long as a sound building could be obtained cheaply. After several other attempts, Northern Counties Housing Association found and converted Granby House into flats, with the help of an Urban Development Grant.

The outcome
50 one bedroom and 11 two bedroom flats were created and subsequently sold to owner occupiers.

Figure 22: The entrance to Granby House flats

Organisation and management of the project

INCUBATION STAGE

Driving force
The Granby House flats owe their existence to the patience, energy and persuasiveness of Eric Lee, the Regional Development Officer of Northern Counties Housing Association. He had long been a supporter of housing rehabilitation and has persuaded Northern Counties to undertake such schemes. He also wanted to do something to help regenerate the centre of Manchester and became very keen to convert large warehouses into low-cost flats.

Objective
Northern Counties is a large, growing housing association (see p. 76 with its headquarters in Manchester which has specialised in fair rent and shared ownership housing schemes. In recent years, when there have been reductions in public funding for housing associations, it has been developing more and more properties for sale and has always been on the look-out for new schemes to keep its programmes going. Eric Lee wished to involve Northern Counties in a major city centre conversion, but he wanted to be sure to select a project which would succeed.

Formulating the scheme
Eric Lee worked out the basis of the scheme before looking seriously at any buildings. Although this was a pioneering type of project, he approached it in a methodical professional way, tying up as much of the details as possible in advance and resisting the temptation to cut corners through enthusiasm.

The essence of the scheme was to develop flats for sale, and this would make it possible to bring in private institutional finance – such as a building society which might then become involved in providing mortgages to the individual purchasers. This type

Figure 21: An Edwardian cotton warehouse converted into Housing Association flats

of conversion scheme, which was an extension of the conventional, or 'institutional' approach to property development, was already becoming fashionable in London, but the great difference was that flat prices there were very much higher. In Manchester where building costs were just as high but selling prices much lower, some form of subsidy would be required. Eric Lee thought that Urban Development Grant was the most likely candidate and he approached Manchester City Council who were positive. On the private sector side Nationwide Building Society were very interested. There was one further detail. The development of housing for sale with the use of private funding could not be carried out by a registered housing association (see p. 77) and so a non-registered housing association (Northern Counties Provident Housing Association) had to be set up. While all these arrangements were being carefully worked out Eric Lee was also looking for the right building.

Selecting the building

Granby House was the fourth building in the Whitworth Street Conservation Area that Eric Lee studied in detail. To him, selecting the right building and obtaining it on the right terms were of the utmost importance; where institutional finance was involved it was necessary to understand and follow the unwritten rules. In each case structural surveys were carried out followed by feasibility and market studies. Indications of the purchase price of the building were obtained and full funding proposals prepared. The first three buildings although potentially viable each failed somewhere along the route. When Granby House came onto the market in early 1983 it looked a natural winner. It was in good condition; its shape and window arrangement (figure 21) made a light well unnecessary; it was also high on Manchester City Council's priority list of buildings. Nevertheless Eric Lee insisted upon going through the same thorough appraisal.

An architect and a builder were invited to prepare and cost a scheme. Northern Counties' own quantity surveyors and marketing department made detailed investigations. Given a building purchase price of just over £200,000 the total cost of the project would be £1 million, or rather more than £16,000 per flat. The average selling price for a one bedroom flat in Manchester was reckoned to be £11,000 (compared to £25,000 or more in London at that time).

NEGOTIATION STAGE

Obtaining the building on good terms

The prices being asked for buildings in Manchester were quite high, based on hope value rather than existing use value. The lowest price which Eric Lee could achieve through negotiation was £210,000 (£3 per sq.ft.). He thought this was too high but realised that with the proposed Urban Development Grant he could make the project work. He therefore agreed the price, subject to obtaining the Urban Development Grant.

Obtaining the finance

Nationwide Building Society agreed to put up £703,000, at 2% above their normal rates because of the experimental nature of the scheme. Manchester City Council were pleased to support an application for £300,000 from Urban Development Grant, which was approved and the building was purchased at the end of 1983.

Selecting a reliable contractor

At this point the builder on whose estimate the whole scheme was based went into liquidation, and so a new contractor had to be found. Caution prevailed. It was decided to go for a fixed price 'design and build' contract (see p. 112) with a major building firm, and to appoint an external project manager to oversee the building works. These steps would lessen the risk of Northern Counties getting into difficulties if anything else went wrong.

From several competitors Fairclough's tender was chosen, but the cost had now risen to nearly £1.3 million, partly because of the new contract arrangements and partly because of the extension of VAT on building alterations in the 1984 budget. As Granby House was a listed building the contractors eventually became exempt from this new tax, but they could still not claim back any VAT they had paid to their suppliers, and so they had to pass most of it on.

Raising more finance

When the new contract was agreed a fresh application for Urban Development Grant had to be made. Nationwide felt that they could not increase their investment because it was linked to unchanged valuations, and so the new ratio of public to private funds had to be higher than before, even though Northern Counties were prepared to invest some of their own resources.

Nationwide took the lead in seeing this revised grant application through because they wished to see this innovative project succeed. £601,000 was applied for, including a contingency of £50,000. However, in the event, only £575,000 was actually taken up. It took several months to get approval, and site work could only start in August 1984.

Sources of finance

	£
Nationwide Building Society	703,000
UDG (75% DoE)	431,000
(25% City of Manchester)	144,000
Northern Counties Own Resources	412,000
	£1,690,000

Figure 23: Granby House promotional brochure

Maintaining financial flexibility

Urban Development Grant is intended to provide just the amount of money needed to turn a non-profitable scheme into a profitable one. It also has provisions which allow money to be clawed back if the scheme turns out to be excessively profitable. The result is to limit the financial flexibility of a scheme, unless contingency payments have been built in. In order to minimise their own risk Northern Counties entered into a fixed price design and build contract. This avoided most, but not all, of the problems. For example, towards the end of the building works, a new chief fire officer was appointed who insisted on certain extra precautions being taken. Although these did not cost a great deal in themselves, they prevented the sale of flats taking place in phases, and delayed planned cash inflows by up to three months. Fortunately Northern Counties Housing Association was able to stand behind the Provident Association and enable it to raise a small bridging loan.

CONSTRUCTION STAGE

Project management

Fairclough's undertook the direct supervision and management of the construction work as part of their fixed price contract. Originally Northern Counties intended that one of their project managers would oversee the building project. However, after the original contractor's banckruptcy, they decided to appoint an outside firm, Peter O'Hare Associates, to look after their interests on the site.

MANAGEMENT STAGE

Marketing

The flats were sold on 125-year leases. Marketing was undertaken jointly by Northern Counties and a firm of local estate agents. An attractive brochure was produced, and the estate agents publicised the flats in the normal way (figure 23). The brochure emphasised the central location of Granby House and the high standard of the refurbishment and the fittings. Priority was given to first time buyers.

Because of the delays that had taken place since the marketing estimates had been made in 1983, and because of the attractiveness of the finished scheme, it was found that substantially higher prices could be obtained than originally foreseen. Most of the flats were quickly sold raising a total of £1.1 million. Even so this did not cover the full cost of the project proving that some form of subsidy was indeed necessary.

Continuing management

Since the flats were sold on long leases the management of Granby House was very standard. Northern Counties already had its own property management department and had no trouble in taking on the management of Granby House.

Notes

Housing Association. A non-profit organisation run by a voluntary committee to provide housing for the benefit of the community or, in some cases, for the benefit of its members. Many housing associations provide housing let at fair (controlled) rents. Some also provide housing for purchase. To be eligible to receive public funding under the Housing Act 1974 associations must be **registered with,** and supervised by, the **Housing Corporation.**

Project references

PROJECT ADDRESS	Granby House, 61/63 Granby Row, Manchester
CONTACT	Eric Lee, Northern Counties Housing Association Ltd., Television House, Mount Street, Manchester M2 5PS Telephone: 061 832-8757
PROJECT ARCHITECTS	The John Cottam Partnership 34 Hall Street, St. Helens, Merseyside WA10 1DL

10 Pipers Court

Old Foundry Road, Ipswich

19th Century clothing factory now re-used as housing. Developed by a private individual in collaboration with a housing association, using public and private finance.

GOOD PRACTICES HIGHLIGHTED

- Driving force
- Obtaining Local Authority Support
- Formulating the Scheme
- Keeping Control of Time

An example of an entrepreneurial approach to the provision of "fair rent" housing in which the local authority and a housing association were closely involved. Although a substantial Improvement Grant was obtained the funding was basically conventional, but problems were avoided by the housing association agreeing to buy the flats. A good example of cooperation between the private, public and voluntary sectors.

Key Facts

Original Building	Type:	Clothing factory
	Construction:	Brick
	Date:	1885 with later additions
	Size:	43,000 sq.ft.
	Storeys:	4
	Location:	Town Centre
	Configuration:	Long and deep
	Condition:	Sound
Concept	New Use:	Public and private flats
	Developer:	Entrepreneur
	Approach:	Entrepreneurial (with conventional funding)
	Manager:	Housing Association
Finance	Public Sector:	£580,000
	Private.Sector:	£1,370,000
Devel-opment	Tenure:	Freehold
	Acquisition Cost:	£250,000
	Conversion Cost:	£1,700,000
	Date of Scheme:	1982–1983
	Lettable Area:	35,500 sq.ft.
	Cost per sq.ft. (gross):	£45.30 (1986 Equivalent: £52.10)*
	Cost per sq.ft. (net):	£54.90 (1986 Equivalent: £63.10)*
Result	No. of Units:	103 flats
	Employment:	Not relevant

*Adjusted for building cost inflation to approximate 1986 value

Figure 24: The clothing factory and fronting offices

PROJECT SUMMARY

The building

Pipers Court has been fashioned out of the old Phillips and Piper clothing factory, a prominent, 4 storey Victorian building with later additions, situated near the centre of Ipswich (figure 24). The building was deep as well as long. Its front was crescent shaped, and it was hemmed in by busy roads. While there was plenty of light along each side the interiors were dark.

Figure 25: The new housing: part rental and partly owner occupied

Figure 26: The basic interior was suitable for adaptation, but not without problems

The problem

The factory reached its heyday making uniforms during the two world wars. Over 800 people were once employed there. Subsequently the business declined and eventually the owner decided to go out of business and sell the building. There was no real demand for a large industrial building on a cramped site. However in Ipswich, as in many other large towns, there was a shortage of rented housing for single people near the centre. As rents were low there was little likelihood of it being provided by new building. Could conversion of an existing building fill the gap?

The scheme

Ron Howarth, a builder-entrepreneur who had recently returned from abroad, bought the building and took up the challenge to build flats. This involved adding new floors, sinking an underground car park, as well as constructing lightwells, corridors, partitions and false ceilings. A housing association which would manage the completed scheme was identified and involved. The local authority supported the scheme and helped co-ordinate the funding.

The outcome

The whole scheme was carried out very quickly. The housing association agreed to buy the 79 fair rent flats, and 24 other flats were sold for owner occupation (figure 25). The exterior was cleaned and the interior enlivened by many attractive touches. After just fourteen months a building that might have been demolished became an attractive feature with a useful purpose.

The organisation and management of the project

INCUBATION STAGE

Driving force

Pipers Court was a complicated scheme. Not only was

there a great deal of conversion work to be done, but also the financing and management arrangements were complex. Yet the scheme went through remarkably quickly. The man chiefly responsible for this was Ron Howarth, a larger-than-life Liverpudlian with considerable construction management experience, who in 1982 had just returned from the Middle East and was looking for a challenge. He bought the building and took the risks, and he indeed was the driving force. However he received a lot of help from others – notably his architects, Ipswich Borough Council and the Orbit Housing Association – all of whom were complete strangers to him at the start of the project. It was part of Ron Howarth's strength that he was able to motivate other people and to gain their confidence and collaboration.

Objectives

Ron Howarth was looking for something to do. The Pipers Court building was brought to his attention when it was up for sale and he felt that it was too good to be scrapped. His original inclination was to convert it into terraced town houses for sale. This would have avoided the necessity of organising long term management. Ipswich Borough Council on the other hand were keen to have flats. They were aware of the growing problem of homelessness among young single people for whom there was nowhere suitable in the town centre. They suggested involving Orbit Housing Association, a large housing association (see p. 112) with an office in Ipswich which might subsequently manage the scheme. Ron Howarth did not mind modifying his ideas, so long as the Council gave him its full support.

Selecting the building

Ron Howarth liked the building. He liked its architecture, its size and its location; no other development sites were available close to the centre of Ipswich. It was an ideal vehicle for a person who wanted to do something that would have impact. The building did have some draw backs (figure 26). It was deep as well as long, the ceilings were too high and there was no spare space on the site. Conversion would be tricky, but because of his experience this aspect did not worry him unduly.

Finding appropriate professionals

Through the estate agents who were selling the building, Ron Howarth was introduced to Roderick Begg of MWT Architects, who already had ideas about Pipers Court, and after discussing the possibilities they decided to work together on it. After making some very preliminary sketches Roderick Begg suggested that the first thing to do was to go and speak to the Council's Housing Department.

Obtaining local authority support

The attitude and support of the Council were crucial to the success of Pipers Court. Once it was agreed that the scheme would cater primarily for young single tenants, the Council was not only supportive but almost became part of the development team. This proved extremely useful. Planning permission was obtained without delay; there was assistance with fire and building regulations and with the grant application, and the whole scheme made very rapid progress.

'When the political wind is in your favour, it is amazing how quickly things get blown along.'

As Ipswich was not an area in which Urban Programme funding was available (see Appendix D) the Council suggested that an application should be made to the DoE for a substantial Housing Improvement Grant (under the Housing Act 1974). In order to be eligible for such a grant the flats would have to be let at fair rates (See p. 83). While it was Ron Howarth's scheme as he owned the building, and took the risk, it was also the Council's scheme, as they were getting the fair rent flats which they wanted. Indeed both parties felt that they had found a formula for collaboration which could be applied to future conversions.

Formulating the scheme

With this basic outline in mind MWT Architects began to design the scheme in more detail. They found that the large internal spaces could be made into properly proportioned flats by altering floor and ceiling heights internally while leaving the outside of the building unchanged. Thus a new ground floor could be created four feet above pavement level, and this in turn would enable a car park to be built underneath the ground floor. A new top storey could be added to create penthouses. Lightwells could open up the centre of the building, and the long interior corridors could be made to look like outdoor pathways. By doing all this a very dense development of 103 flats and maisonettes could be given an attractive and homely feeling.

The cost of doing all this would be high, and so Ron Howarth prepared a feasibility study which took into account the likely level of fair rents (which would have to be adhered to for at least the first five years under the rules which govern Improvement Grants) and the cost and timing of conversion. The outcome appeared favourable so long as a substantial grant could be obtained, and the indications for that were favourable. So Ron Howarth set up a development company, Construction (UK) Ltd., to buy the building and convert it.

At an early stage it was agreed that Orbit Housing Association would take on the management of the flats when they were ready for occupation. They took an active part in the design of the scheme, making suggestions, for example about the materials to be used, based on their management experience. This early involvement and commitment made the subsequent transfer of the driving force role to Orbit straightforward.

NEGOTIATION STAGE

Obtaining the building on good terms
It was essential to obtain the freehold of the building in order to attract funding. From the feasibility study Ron Howarth knew what he could afford to pay, and he bought it for £250,000 after outbidding the competitors.

Raising the finance
The conversion costs were estimated at £1.35 million including financial charges. Private funds (10%) and a loan from a merchant bank, Johnson Matthey Bank (90%), were used to buy the building. The Improvement Grant (£580,000) was calculated as 75% of the eligible conversion costs and a further 2-year bridging loan was arranged with the merchant bank, as the local high street banks were not interested in the project. Subsequently costs overran the estimates by 25%, bringing the total project cost to nearly £2.0 million. An extra £350,000 had to be raised in the form of another loan from another merchant bank.

Sources of finance

	£
Personal Resources	25,000
Bridging Loan	995,000
Second Bank Loan	350,000
Improvement Grant (Housing)	580,000
	£1,950,000

This was a conventional approach to funding. Short term finance was raised to cover the construction costs, and the next step would have been to arrange long term finance for the finished scheme and repay the short term loans. However, as with many innovative conversion schemes, it was by no means certain that any financial institution would be prepared to buy it.

Maintaining financial flexibility
The Improvement Grant was useful in that it was available early in the scheme to cover much of the basic work. However, it was not nearly sufficient on its own, and indeed Improvement Grants are intended to cover only a proportion of the eligible costs. Furthermore, the grant did not provide any flexibility, firstly because it committed the scheme to a specified number of flats, to be let at fair rents, and secondly because it had, in principle, to be spent within a financial year which imposed constraints upon the scheduling of the work.

The bridging loan, too, was only short term. It could only be drawn down as certain work was completed and it all had to be repaid within two years. The equity, the flexible risk-money invested in the project, was only £25,000 and it says much for Ron Howarth's entrepreneurial approach that he went into such a scheme with no firm arrangements for long term finance. In the event the collaborative rela-tionships he had developed with Ipswich Borough Council and the Orbit Housing Association enabled the financial equation to be solved.

First the 24 penthouses were sold to a private housing company for £400,000 and then Orbit Housing Society bought the 79 fair rent flats for just under £1 million, £600,000 of which came from an index-linked mortgage (see p. 112) from the Nationwide Building Society, which the Council guaranteed under Section 111 of the 1980 Housing Act. The Council also facilitated the transaction by not requiring the repayment of the Improvement Grant, which they could have done as the building was being sold within five years. It was this collaboration between the public, private and voluntary sectors that finally secured a workable financial package.

CONSTRUCTION STAGE

Project management
An experienced local contractor was employed under a standard JCT contract (see p. 112). Ron Howarth acted as project manager himself. He was on site at the centre of things all day and every day. He took on the architect's plans as his own and galvanised everyone around them. This heightened excitement and commitment. He knew the construction business and he insisted on rapid and direct decisions, which kept the momentum of the project going.

Keeping control of money
In one sense the money was not well controlled. The final costs turned out to be 25% higher than anticipated. In the main this was due to the problems of dealing with a non-rectangular building and of altering the interior floor levels. Additional costs were also incurred when a new Fire Officer took a different view to his predecessor on fire-proofing and fire escapes. This reinforces the view that it is difficult to predict costs precisely on a complex conversion scheme for it is often necessary to make design modifications in order to work round the unexpected.

However, cash flow was well monitored and controlled. This undoubtedly kept the project, which had very little financial flexibility, out of trouble. Ron Howarth's son, who had just left school, devised a personal computer programme which predicted cash inflows (from grant and loan) and cash outflows (to pay contractors, invoices etc.) for a given schedule of operations. Thus as the schedule changed cash shortages could be predicted, and on occasions certain items of work were even delayed in order to keep the cash flow in balance.

Keeping control of time
Ron Howarth first began studying the Pipers Court project in September 1982. Sewing machines were still operating in the old factory in October 1982. Planning permission was granted, and building work started at the end of the year. Ten months later Pipers Court was

officially opened by a Minister from the Department of the Environment, and the first of 103 occupants began moving in. The total time from start to finish was only fourteen months. By any standards this was a very short development time. It required detailed scheduling and firm control. Everyone worked to scheduled deadlines. Even so Ron Howarth had originally planned for the building works to take only six months. The main reasons for the extension were the wet weather during March and April 1983 while the main roof was off, changes in fire requirements, and difficulties in dealing with the cresent shaped building. But when delay occurred, the work schedules were revised, new targets were agreed and the cash flow implications were checked.

It is often said that building projects, and particularly conversions, take a long time to conceive, assemble the resource for and carry out. In this case, a complicated and innovative scheme took little over a year. The two factors that enabled this to happen were a driving force who worked hard and galvanised others and a very positive local authority which did its best to co-ordinate others and overcome problems.

MANAGEMENT STAGE

Marketing and continuing management
The 24 penthouses were marketed by another housing company, Barratts, which bought them all from Construction (UK) Ltd. The 79 fair rent flats needed no marketing at all. The local authority nominated single people from its housing list for half of them, and the rest were filled by people on Orbit's list. As explained above, Orbit bought all the fair rent flats and took on the management of Pipers Court as planned all along. Thus Ron Howarth was able to pass on the driving force role to those who were equally committed to the continuing success of the scheme.

Pipers Court is regarded as a great success, providing fair rent housing for single people in a town centre, where new building would have been prohibitively expensive. Because of the cost overruns Construction (UK) Ltd. only broke even on the project, and it has been subsequently learned that conversions of industrial buildings for housing receive 50% Improvement Grants, not 75%. This will make future schemes more difficult.

Notes

Fair Rent: A controlled rent (for housing) set by a local authority Rent Officer in order to stop private landlords overcharging their tenants. Most tenants in private housing have the legal right to apply for a fair rent, which is likely to be below the free market rent. It is a condition of the DoE's Improvement Grants that only fair rents are charged for at least the first five years if a grant aided property is let.

Index-Linked Mortgages: A rare type of mortgage which has a low rate of interest, say 4% per year, but the amount of capital which is repaid each year over the life of the loan increases in line with inflation. The effect of this is that the annual repayments start low but increase over time. But, of course, the rental income from which the mortgage repayments have to come, should also increase over time.

Project references

PROJECT ADDRESS	Pipers Court, 30 Old Foundry Road, Ipswich IP4 2AJ Telephone: 0473–50874
CONTACT	David Simmons, Orbit Housing Association
PROJECT ARCHITECTS	MWT Architects Ltd., 32 Silent Street, Ipswich IP1 1TG.

11 Bradbury Street

Bradbury Street, London N16

A row of derelict shops and houses, now re-used as shops, workshops and offices for small co-operatives. Developed by a co-operative development agency, using Urban Programme funding.

GOOD PRACTICES HIGHLIGHTED

- Driving force
- Selecting the Building
- Finding Appropriate Professionals
- Obtaining Local Authority Support
- Continuing Management

Commitment to a cause, which was translated into a practical end result, enabled a totally inexperienced community group to obtain and redevelop a row of shops in inner London, overcoming extraordinary obstacles on the way. Although highly unconventional in some respects the scheme succeeded because the group got most of the basic points right and they have since carried out other property schemes.

Key Facts

Original Building	*Type:*	Terraced housing and shops
	Construction:	Brick
	Date:	Victorian
	Size:	15,000 sq.ft.
	Storeys:	3
	Location:	Inner city
	Configuration:	Long and thin
	Condition:	Very bad
Concept	*New Use:*	Shops and Offices
	Developer:	Hackney Co-operative Developments
	Approach:	Entrepreneurial
	Manager:	Hackney Co-operative Developments
Finance	*Public Sector:*	£322,000
	Private Sector:	£ 4,000
Development	*Tenure:*	10-year lease
	Acquisition Cost:	Nil
	Conversion Cost:	£326,000
	Date of Scheme:	1981–1984
	Lettable Area:	10,250 sq.ft.
	Cost per sq.ft. (gross):	£21.75 (1986 Equivalent: £25.00)*
	Cost per sq.ft. (net):	£31.80 (1986 Equivalent: £37.00)*
Result	*No. of Units:*	18
	Employment:	80

*Adjusted for building cost inflation to approximate 1986 value

Figure 27: The derelict shops and houses in Bradbury Street in 1981

PROJECT SUMMARY

The building

Bradbury Street is a small road off Kingsland High Street, a busy secondary shopping centre in Hackney, East London. The building was a row of 10 little shops with living accommodation above, owned by the Greater London Council and, in 1981, derelict and due to be demolished to provide car parking. Its attraction was that it was a whole row of shops, which would normally be impossible for a voluntary organisation to obtain.

The problem

Hackney Co-operative Developments (HCD) was a small group set up to foster worker co-operatives in Hackney. Its mission was to prove that co-ops could succeed and ought to be taken as seriously as any other type of business organisation. HCD knew that it was difficult for co-ops to obtain good premises. Well-located shops like Bradbury Street could give a great boost to the whole co-op movement. The problem was that HCD did not own the building, had no money or experience and, being part of the co-operative movement, had little external credibility. The building was in very poor condition and could only be obtained on a short term basis.

The scheme

The scheme involved raising substantial funds, converting the building rapidly into shops, workshops and offices and finding tenants. Enough Urban Programme money was obtained to refurbish the shops, and later further funds were raised to complete the project using building co-ops.

The outcome

The shops and workshops were finished in March 1983 and quickly let. The offices followed in 1984. All the tenants were co-ops. 16 out of the original 18 are still in business and pay independently-assessed market rents. HCD continues to manage the building and has since undertaken other successful developments. It is planning to start negotiations with Hackney Council over the provision of a longer lease.

Organisation and management of the project

INCUBATION STAGE

Driving force

It took some time for Hackney Co-operative Developments (HCD) to come round to the idea of property development. But when it did it undertook the Bradbury Street project with such zeal that all obstacles and inexperience were overcome. HCD had been set up in 1979 to promote worker co-operatives (see p. 89) in Hackney. It was already fully stretched providing advice and support to its clients when, in late 1981, one of its members drew attention to Bradbury Street

Figure 28: By 1984 activity had returned to the rehabilitated shops and upstairs offices

Figure 29: Inside an upstairs architect's office

and urged HCD to develop it. Obtaining premises was a major difficulty for co-ops. They were treated with suspicion; landlords did not take them as serious businesses and did not like dealing with them. One of the best ways HCD could help co-ops was by providing premises for them.

In theory in a co-op all decisions are made communally, but in practice different groups or individuals may take a lead at different times. In this case there was a strong commitment, shared by all HCD's Steering Group, to making co-ops succeed. The conversion of Bradbury Street into premises specially for co-ops was recognised as an important step towards that goal. A small sub-committee called the Property Working Group was set up, and although its membership varied over time it became the driving force behind the Bradbury Street scheme. It was involved in all aspects of the project, not only in the development phase but right through into property management, with an overriding concern for the success of the occupants.

Objectives

HCD's objective of proving that co-ops could succeed and should be taken seriously focussed attention onto the future use of the building, not just its conversion. HCD wanted Bradbury Street to become a showcase for co-ops. It intended to stay involved in Bradbury Street, managing the building and providing advice and support to its tenants. Furthermore those tenants would pay a reasonable rent, which in turn would enable HCD to build up a fund to provide start-up capital or financial support for yet more co-operatives. Thus the successful end-use of Bradbury Street was all important, and it created a strong sense of mission for the project.

> 'We were a very diverse group, but we had few arguments as we were all so involved and committed. I have never had such an exciting time as that.'

Selecting the building

When HCD accepted the idea of property development, it decided it should look at other buildings in Hackney apart from Bradbury Street. Indeed Bradbury Street had many drawbacks. It was in a terrible condition; even the structural engineer who had been asked to look it over refused to go upstairs. It was the worst set of buildings he had ever seen (figure 27). Also the local council's plan was to demolish the building and council plans are not easy to change. However, Bradbury Street also had great advantages. It was in a good business location, especially for shops, and it was probably a unique opportunity to obtain a whole group of shops together. Bradbury Street was the best building available for the achievement of HCD's objectives.

Formulating the scheme

The outline of the scheme was clear. The ground floor units would naturally make shops or workshops (figure 28). The upper floors would make offices or studios (figure 29). HCD knew that these were the types of premises that co-ops required, and these uses suited the Bradbury Street building ideally.

Finding appropriate professionals

One of HCD's workers, Janet Keighley, realised the urgent need for professional advice, but HCD had no money to pay for it. However she had a contact who worked for Franklin Stafford, architects who already had experience in conversion and rehabilitation. They gave free advice and a rough estimate of the basic conversion costs, £30 per sq.ft. They also pointed out that the work could be done in two phases: first the basic structural work and shop refurbishment; afterwards the conversion of the upper floors. No detailed feasibility study was done, but this information was enough for HCD to start discussions with Hackney Council.

Later, when detailed designs were required, the Steering Group felt that it was vital to have experienced yet sympathetic architects chosen on a rational basis. As they did not know the architectural world well they approached the Royal Institute of British Architects (see p. 89) which recommended a short list of suitably experienced firms. From that list HCD again chose Franklin Stafford and asked them to design, cost and manage the work.

NEGOTIATION STAGE

Obtaining Local Authority support

HCD already had good links with Hackney Council. It had been established with council backing. Now Hackney's Planning Department and Economic Development Unit (EDU) supported the idea of re-using Bradbury Street if it were at all possible, and helped HCD to apply for funding.

Raising the finance

HCD had no money or assets of its own and, because of the way co-ops were regarded, virtually no prospect of raising any finance from the private sector. Funding, therefore, had to come entirely from the public sector. It happened that there was underspending in the 1982-83 Urban Programme, and so money was available for additional projects. Also the Department of the Environment was keen to encourage capital, as opposed to revenue, projects by voluntary sector bodies. The Bradbury Street proposal suited the requirements perfectly, and so with detailed costings from Franklin Stafford an Urban Programme grant of £200,000 was obtained (£190,000 for the building works and £10,000 for HCD's administration), on condition that it was spent by March 1983.

This would enable Phase 1 of the scheme to be carried out. Funding for Phase 2 could not be guaranteed at this stage, but had to be applied for as part of the following year's Urban Programme (1983–84) and in due course a second grant of £109,700 was obtained.

Selecting a reliable contractor

Speed was vital. The first phase had to be completed in a few months or the grant would be lost. HCD naturally wanted the work to be done by co-ops, but in the circumstances it was prepared to be flexible and to give way on this point of principle and select a large, established building firm which could guarantee to finish the job on time. At this stage only one matter was still outstanding, the ownership of the building.

Obtaining the building on good terms

In 1982 the GLC transferred most of its housing stock to local London boroughs. Unfortunately the files on Bradbury Street got lost for several months during this process. Eventually Hackney obtained the freehold, but it took nearly three more years to agree a lease with HCD. The Valuer's Department felt duty bound to obtain the best terms possible for the Borough, and to safeguard its rights to future development. It therefore wished to include conditions in the lease which HCD felt would penalise its tenants and make it difficult to manage the building properly.

As time was running out, HCD had to sign a Building Agreement in November 1982 in order to be allowed to start the conversion work. In effect they were agreeing to be bound by a lease the terms of which would be decided in the future, and indeed a 10-year lease was not signed until one year after the conversion was complete and the tenants had moved in. No conventional developer would start site works until his ownership rights were clearly defined. However, since HCD had no direct financial stake in the scheme, and because of its good relations with other parts of Hackney Council, it felt it could take this unconventional approach. The subsequent costs in management time and legal fees, however, were high. Thus although Hackney Council was basically in favour of the scheme because of its economic and environmental impact, different departments with different perspectives had different views about what constituted real benefit to the Borough. This shows how important it is for all parts of a local authority to have a similar perspective if local economic development is to be effective.

Maintaining flexibility

HCD had no financial flexibility. The grant rules forced them into a rigid timetable. Their wish to employ co-ops whenever possible imposed extra constraints. However their great strength was their commitment to the end result, which in turn drew similar commitments from others. Thus some flexibility both with regard to the work done and the way of doing it was possible. The Council, the architects, the contractors and HCD themselves were all prepared to act unconventionally in order to finish the work on time and within budget. In fact there were small cost over-runs in each phase. The first was met by a small grant from Hackney, and the second from

88

income which by then was beginning to flow in from tenants.

Sources of finance

		£
Urban Programme (75% DoE)		236,000
	(25% Hackney)	79,000
Additional Grant – Hackney Council		7,000
Rental Income		4,000
		£326,000

CONSTRUCTION STAGE

Keeping control of time and money

Phase 1, the basic structural work and the refurbishment of the ground floor shops, was completed on time and within budget. The architects supervised the contractors conventionally. Some additional, unforeseen work had to be done, but this was compensated for by leaving out other items. With fixed grants, cash limits are the real controls and Franklin Stafford understood this well. Due to the speed at which the job was done some faults showed up later which caused extra maintenance expense. As they were not directly involved in site supervision in Phase 1, HCD subsequently felt that some of the original work was not done with sufficient care. The architects, however, felt that any problems were due to the short-life nature of the work specified.

Project management

As the project progressed Janet Keighley became in effect the full time project manager, doing the day to day work under the direction of the Property Working Group. During Phase 1, she was fully occupied with such matters as grant and lease negotiation, finding and selecting tenants, planning Phase 2, monitoring progress, discussing changes and reporting back to the group. This was a very necessary job. The client, even if a voluntary organisation, has an active part to play.

On Phase 2 there was even more to be done. As the building work consisted mostly of fitting out the upper floors and was not quite so rushed, it was possible to split it up and parcel it out to small building co-ops. All building co-ops in London were invited to apply and eight were eventually chosen. This satisfied HCD's requirement to employ co-ops whenever possible, but added a complication which other developers would avoid. HCD employed a site supervisor, who not only organised and supervised the work but gave technical help where needed. He, rather than the architects, became responsible for approving the quality of the work done which led to complications over certification of the work. Also the administration became more time consuming with no fewer than 82 staged payments having to be made in Phase 2, compared with 4 in Phase 1. Even though HCD's special requirements complicated the situation, it would still have been necessary to have one person managing the project virtually full time. Project management took far more time and effort than anticipated, which emphasises the need to make adequate provision for this, and to have adequate funding.

MANAGEMENT STAGE

Marketing
From its direct contacts with co-ops, HCD had known all along that there would be ample demand for space in Bradbury Street. Indeed it has subsequently taken on three more buildings. One advantage of being able to identify specific tenants in advance is that their special requirements can sometimes be incorporated into the building work, which makes for a stronger landlord and tenant bond.

Continuing management
As with many community organisations, HCD faced a potential conflict of interest between being a landlord and wanting to support its tenants. However as HCD had no spare resources, Bradbury Street had to be managed commercially, but with two special features. First, reasonable market rents (plus a service charge) are independently assessed by a commercial estate agent and must be paid monthly by standing order. Secondly, HCD has a written Tenant Arrears Policy which prospective tenants have carefully explained to them and which they have to sign before their leases are finalised.

A few tenants have had problems paying their rents, but this is not uncommon with start-ups especially in a disadvantaged inner city area. However, HCD had had the ability and willingness to intervene, and it is widely appreciated that if it had not been for HCD and its pioneering efforts few of its tenant co-ops would have been in business at all.

Notes

Co-operatives. A worker's co-operative is a business which is owned and controlled by all those who work in it. Decisions are made on the principle that every worker has one vote and only workers vote. The profits made belong to the business generally and not to individuals within it.

Royal Institute of British Architects (RIBA). The professional body for architects in Britain, it exists primarily to promote the interests of its members but can act as a source of information for those new to property conversion who need to be put in touch with local architects with relevant experience. Contact either the Community Architecture Department, or the Client Advisory Service, 66 Portland Place, London W1 (01–580 5533).

Project references

PROJECT ADDRESS CONTACT	4–10a Bradbury Street, London N16
	Hackney Co-operative Developments, 16 Dalston Lane, London E8 3AZ. Telephone: 01–254 4829
PROJECT ARCHITECTS	Franklin Stafford Partnership, 2 Acklam Road, London W10

12 Camden Lock

Chalk Farm Road, London NW1

Victorian stables and warehouse, now re-used as craft workshops, market, restaurants, dance hall and centre for cultural events. Developed by individuals using private finance.

GOOD PRACTICES HIGHLIGHTED

- Driving force
- Entrepreneurial Approach
- Formulating the Scheme
- Maintaining Flexibility
- Keeping Control of Time and Money
- Marketing
- Continuing Management

One of the most famous developments in London in recent years. A classic example of an entrepreneurial approach to development with special attention paid to attracting users and to creating excitement. Also an example of how the initiative and drive behind a scheme can be transferred from one person to another during the project, thus enabling different personal characteristics to come to the fore at different stages.

Key Facts

Original Building	*Type:*	Stables and Ware-house
	Construction:	Brick
	Date:	Victorian
	Size:	0.75 acre
	Storeys:	1, 2 and 3
	Location:	By canal, in inner city
	Configuration:	Buildings round courtyards
	Condition:	Neglected but usable
Concept	*New Use:*	Workshops/Market/ Entertainments
	Developer:	Three individuals
	Approach:	Entrepreneurial
	Manager:	One of the developers
Finance	*Public Sector:*	Nil
	Private Sector:	£70,000
Devel-opment	*Tenure:*	7 year lease initially
	Acquisition Cost:	£10,000
	Conversion Cost:	£60,000
	Date of Scheme:	1971 onwards
	Lettable Area:	27,000 sq.ft.
	Cost per sq.ft. (gross):	Not relevant
	Cost per sq.ft. (net):	£2.60 (1986 Equivalent: £10.00)*
Result	*No. of Units:*	50 plus weekend market
	Employment:	400

*Adjusted for building cost inflation to approximate 1986 value

91

PROJECT SUMMARY

The buildings
An unpromising group of warehouses and former canal stables clustered round three cobbled yards and a small basin on the Regent's Canal in what was then a run down, mainly residential area of inner London.

The problem
The canal had fallen into virtual disuse. The horses had long gone and the stables were used by a firm of packing case makers which, in 1971, was going out of business. The wider area was equally drab being blighted by a proposed motorway.

The scheme
Two friends who had previously been converting residential property bought the site as they wanted to extend their activities to commercial buildings as well. They liked the canal and the site was cheap. They took a gamble that the motorway blight might eventually be lifted but in the meantime they looked for short life uses such as craft workshops, a weekend market, restaurants, a dance hall, boat trips and events held on and around the canal. Great effort was put into attracting people to the site.

The outcome
By the time that the blight was lifted in 1976, Camden Lock had become famous, particularly for its weekend market and there was strong local opposition to redevelopment. Eventually proposals based on extending the existing uses were approved. Thus what had originally been intended as short term uses became permanent and one of London's well known tourist attractions.

Organisation and management of the project

INCUBATION STAGE

Objectives
Camden Lock is a classic example of an opportunistic, entrepreneurial approach to development. It is not a case of implementing a well thought out plan, but of looking for and reacting to opportunities within a framework. In fact there was a specific plan originally, but it has been developed and changed with experience.

In 1971 Northside Developments Ltd., a company formed by school friends Peter Wheeler (a surveyor) and Bill Fulford (a doctor) to buy and convert houses, initially on the north side of Clapham Common, was looking for a site for a commercial development. The two partners liked the canal site and thought it had potential. They bought the remaining 7-year lease cheaply, reckoning that they would be able to extend it, and they gambled that the motorway scheme which was blighting the area would be dropped, leaving them with an opportunity for long term development.

Meanwhile it was necessary to do something with the site. At the very least it must earn enough to cover its rent and rates. The obvious thing to do was to find some immediate uses, which could be easily removed if the motorway really did come, and from which experience could be gained. This is how Camden Lock was born.

Driving force
Camden Lock has gone through all the stages in its development and three people, Peter Wheeler, Bill Fulford and Eric Reynolds, can claim to have been the

Figure 30: The whole area was by 1971 run down and becoming derelict

Figure 31: By 1976 the renovation was underway and life returning to the locks, light industry arriving first

driving force at different times. Their ability to work together and to hand the initiative on from one to another was remarkable and has made an important contribution to the success of the project. At different times different characteristics were required to run the project and they managed to pass the driving force on without losing impetus. Peter Wheeler was the original deal-maker. Bill Fulford was the consolidator and organiser. Jointly they put together the development plans and organised the new uses. Eric Reynolds has been the hands-on promoter and manager of activity, especially the weekend market and other events.

All three saw the site and the buildings in the same way, as a means to an end: a means for attracting enough people and activity to at least pay for itself. It had to be changed from a derelict backwater into a place of activity and if possible into a place of excitement, which in turn would generate more activity. They shared the same enthusiasm for making things happen. They talked a lot among themselves about their ideas, and each allowed the others to follow through what they were good at.

Selecting the building

Peter Wheeler believed that the buildings and the site at Camden Lock had potential but potential for what, in the short term, he did not really know. The location was good, not far from the prosperous core of London, but the blight and shabbiness tended to disguise this fact (figure 30). Most of the buildings could be re-used relatively easily. Also the price was low, and so even if the property did not have a long term future it was worth buying.

Formulating the scheme

The scheme evolved. The overall objective was to generate activity and attract people. The first step was just to clear up the site and repaint the buildings. The stables provided small units naturally. The site was already zoned for light industrial use. The simplest thing to do was to start letting the space as craft workshops (figure 31). It soon became clear that it was easy to attract tenants so long as they were only required to commit to a short stay. At Camden Lock workshops could be rented by the week if necessary – a quite revolutionary idea at the time. Immediately the spaces filled up and immediately there was a positive cash flow, which enabled money to be spent on the bigger buildings and on ways of attracting potential customers for the craft workshops onto the site.

Food seemed an obvious way of attracting people, and so the next idea was to start converting some of the buildings into restaurants. In contrast to the craft businesses which might be here to-day and gone tomorrow, restaurants would be more permanent and would set the tone of the place. Therefore great care was taken to select the right type of restaurants with the right management. Northside even went so far as to set up partnerships with each of the operators, not only to help them with their capital investments but

also to ensure some control over how the restaurants were managed. One in fact became a dance hall. No rent was charged until they began to find their feet.

Next, ideas for the cobbled yards were discussed. Either they could just be used for car parking or, perhaps, as an open market place which might also be an outlet for goods made in the craft workshops. Renting out stalls was not too onerous a task, yet it soon transformed Camden Lock, and indeed the whole of Camden High Street into which the weekend market eventually overflowed

At the same time, to ensure the success of all these good ideas, it was important to attract customers to the site especially at weekends. The obvious thing to do was to use the site, and especially the part along the water, for well publicised weekend events. Dances, concerts, special interest group events, performances of all kinds were organised and widely advertised on local radio and elsewhere. It took a great deal of energy, but it was energy and atmosphere rather than architecture, that were the key. Soon Camden Lock became a great attraction, bringing in people and bringing in cash, some of which in turn could be used to maintain and improve the site. Thus Camden Lock developed by recognising and building on a series of simple opportunities. While the site has been greatly improved since 1971, it is certainly no architectural showpiece; it is just an exciting place to be.

> 'When we started here it was so quiet that you could have literally sat in the middle of Camden High Street reading your Sunday newspaper without any fear of being run over by a car. Now you would get trampled underfoot.'

NEGOTIATION STAGE

Raising the finance

The original 7-year lease cost under £10,000 and was paid for out of Northside's own funds. A considerable amount of conversion work has been carried out over the years, in addition to normal maintenance and refurbishment. This has involved altering the floor level in one building, constructing fire escapes, installing services and erecting temporary buildings. It cost over £60,000 (about £250,000 at 1986 prices) and was financed by Northside itself, using cash flow from operations supplemented by short-term bank borrowings and a medium term mortgage. In addition Northside has invested directly in some of the activities on the site.

By carrying out the scheme incrementally, by building up demand rapidly, and by focussing on activity rather than a high standard of architecture, Camden Lock has been able to generate its own finance.

While profits were modest to start with they have built up substantially over the years, not only because of the extra activities but also because it became possible to attract more stable tenants willing to pay higher rents as Camden Lock became better known. Once the motorway blight was lifted a 125-year lease was negotiated with British Waterways Board and plans were made for a large building on the site of the weekend market. After a long drawn out planning battle, permission has recently been granted for modified proposals. These include some new building while maintaining the market and the present atmosphere of the site. By now the cash flow from operations is so strong that there will be no difficulty in supporting any loan that is required. This illustrates the advantage of developing in phases and of concentrating on cash generation early in the life of a project.

Maintaining flexibility

Flexibility was central to the entrepreneurial approach, but flexibility within general guidelines. Northside knew what it was aiming for – activity, excitement and positive cash flow. It tried to build on opportunities and grow, but always starting anything new in a small and manageable way, and as far as possible, everything had to pay for itself as it went along. It is only after 15 years, with Camden Lock very well established, that major new investment will be made. Throughout, a strictly practical approach has been taken to the spending of money. For example, while the area around the canal basin itself has been greatly improved, large sums of money have not been spent on facelifting the site as it appears from the main road.

CONSTRUCTION AND MANAGEMENT STAGE

Project management

As far as Northside was concerned developing and running Camden Lock were one and the same thing. Buildings were adapted, if necessary, to accommodate a growing use. It was the use that was all important and project management was all about generating more use. The marketing and the management of the site have always been done directly by the developers themselves, with an emphasis on direct informal action. Each focussed on what they were good at. For example, Eric Reynolds, who enjoyed marketing and promotion, used to run the site at weekends when there were frequent events and the market. Bill Fulford and Peter Wheeler used to run the site during the week which required patience in sorting out problems and ensuring good neighbourliness between all the tenants on a crowded site. So all day, all year round, Camden Lock was actively managed, and at different times it became a way of life for each of the driving forces.

Furthermore particular attention has been paid to maintaining good relations with all those who work on the site. There are regular meetings with all the tenants and operators to discuss problems and proposals affecting the site and other matters such as joint promotion.

94

Using professionals

Except on the plans for the new building professionals have been used very sparingly. Peter Wheeler was a surveyor himself and the others felt that common sense was the best guide to the use of a building, and their inclination was to alter the buildings as little as possible. An architect has been used to prepare detailed drawings where necessary and all the conversion work has been carried out by the same family firm of builders, who know the site well.

Keeping control of time and money

Management control at Camden Lock is deceptively informal, but in practice extremely tight. A crowded space and a busy schedule impose fierce disciplines. Some of the planning is still done, literally, on the back of an envelope, but also for each week there is a plan, based on a map of the site, for exactly what is going to happen, where, and how much cash each space will generate. There is a separate plan for each weekend. This is direct, hands-on control of time and money, resulting in little waste of either.

Marketing

When it started out Camden Lock had very little to sell. Even the canal was drab and out of fashion. But step by step it has built itself into a major centre of activity which has led to a remarkable revival of the surrounding area and to others copying it on nearby sites. It all seems magical, but in fact the activities which take place at Camden Lock are fairly mundane – craft workshops, restaurants, a street market – and the advertising budget even now is only £8,000 per year. Yet marketing was the foundation of the success.

Marketing simply means thinking out what potential customers want and organising your operations so as to provide it. Starting with cheap workshop space available for short periods, and right through to restaurants, river trips and the market, that is all that has been done. Beginning from nothing Camden Lock has been turned into a place where people want to be, a place which people want to use. The message has always been 'Come and join in. You will enjoy it.'

Project references

PROJECT ADDRESS	Camden Lock, Chalk Farm Road, London NW1 8AF Telephone: 01-485 7963
CONTACT	Bill Fullford Eric Reynolds Peter Wheeler
PROJECT ARCHITECTS	John Dickinson, Dickinson, Quarme & Associates, Studio 7, Royal Victoria Patriotic Buildings, Fitzhugh Grove, Trinity Road, London SW18 3SX. Telephone: 01-870 8764

13 Canal Museum

Canal Street, Nottingham

Small 19th Century canal warehouse and stables, now re-used as museum, workspace units, pub and restaurant. Local authority development, using public and private finance, including Urban Programme funds.

GOOD PRACTICES HIGHLIGHTED

- Driving force
- Formulating the Scheme
- Maintaining Flexibility
- Using Reliable Contractors
- Continuing Management

A creative, mixed-use scheme in which a local authority played an entrepreneurial role, drawing in both public and private finance and satisfying a range of different objectives on a very small site. In this example the project was broken down into smaller parts, each of which had its own identifiable future income and its own source of finance.

Key Facts

Original Building	Type:	Warehouse, stables
	Construction:	Brick
	Date:	1895
	Size:	17,500 sq.ft.
	Storeys:	Mostly 4
	Location:	By canal, off city centre
	Configuration:	Buildings on courtyard
	Condition:	Structurally sound
Concept	New Use:	Mixed (Museum/Pub/ Workspace)
	Developer:	City Council
	Approach:	Entrepreneurial
	Manager:	Museum staff/ Landlord of pub
Finance	Public Sector:	£124,000
	Private Sector:	£245,000
Development	Tenure:	Freehold
	Acquisition Cost:	Nil
	Conversion Cost:	£369,000
	Date of Scheme:	1979–1982
	Lettable Area:	17,000 sq.ft.
	Cost per sq.ft. (gross):	£21.10 (1986 Equivalent: £28.00)*
	Cost per sq.ft. (net):	£21.70 (1986 Equivalent: £28.60)*
Result	No. of Units:	3 plus Museum, Pub, Restaurant
	Employment:	35

*Adjusted for building cost inflation to approximate 1986 value

PROJECT SUMMARY

The buildings
The Canal Museum site consists of two small ranges of brick buildings dating from 1895 and an attractive cobbled courtyard. It is right next to the Nottingham and Beeston Canal and on the edge of Nottingham city centre. The main 4 storey building used to be a warehouse and has its own basin running right into it. The other buildings which have only 2 storeys used to be offices and stables.

The problem
The canal ceased to be used commercially and fell into disrepair, and the city turned its back on the canalside buildings. This warehouse was fortunate to find use as a council storehouse, and was at least kept secure and watertight, but the site deteriorated and in 1979 a decision had to be made either to demolish the buildings and sell the site or to re-use them in a reasonably commercial way. The buildings were strong and sound, but totally without services and they were slightly off the beaten track.

The scheme
The City Council's Arts Director wanted to use the ground floor of the warehouse with its water access as a canal museum. The upper floors could be converted into craft workshops/industrial units. But to draw more people onto the site, and generate more activity and revenue, something extra was needed, and it was decided to lease the stables and offices to a brewery for conversion into a pub and restaurant. Each part of the scheme was carried out independently but at the same time.

The outcome
The Canal Museum opened in June 1981, the units and the pub/restaurant followed in 1982. The museum is modest but quite well visited and it is going to expand. The environmental improvements have greatly improved the site, and the upper floors yield useful income. The great success of the site is the pub which does a brisk trade, animates the site and sustains the whole project financially.

Organisation and management of the project

INCUBATION STAGE

Driving force
The Nottingham Canal Museum project was devised and implemented by the City Council, using its normal departmental structure. The Planning, Arts and Technical Services Departments all played important parts in the team effort, but the driving force was Jim Taylor, then a middle-ranking planner. It was he who persuaded the officer group to support re-use rather than demolition. It was he who made the application for Urban Programme funding. It was he who came up with the idea of a pub and restaurant to ensure the scheme's commercial viability (although it

Figure 32: The old warehouse offices converted into a pub

Figure 33: The stables now house a brewery and restaurant

96

was Technical Services that pointed out that the pub should be on the road not the canal). It was he who arranged for the Operation Clean Up programme to make the site and surroundings attractive at no extra cost to the project.

Jim Taylor is energetic and enthusiastic, and although he had no property development experience himself he was able to build on the professional property strengths of a local authority and make it act entrepreneurially. Furthermore it was possible to divide up the scheme into four separate parts, each of which could be carried through by someone with a real interest in its successful future use:

- Museum (Arts Director)
- Workshop Units (Technical Services)
- Pub and Restaurant (Whitbreads)
- Environmental Improvements (Planning Department)

Objectives
There were several different objectives involved. The Arts Director wanted a Canal Museum, making use of the fact that the canal came right into the building. The Planning Department wanted to clean up the derelict site as part of a long term plan to improve the canal. Technical Services Department wanted to generate money for the Council. The Council was also keen to develop small industrial units.

In the end a scheme was devised that met all these objectives on a very small site and was financially viable. The key was to break the scheme down into its constituent parts and to work out how to finance and manage each part separately, at minimum cost to the Council. This was a typically entrepreneurial approach.

Selecting the building
In this case the buildings came first. They were already Council owned but in 1979 a definite decision had to be made either to demolish them or to re-use them. The buildings were in sound condition and quite well located, but they lacked services and were surrounded by dereliction. The challenge was to find a viable scheme for re-using them.

Formulating the scheme
The City Council agreed to support a Canal Museum on the ground floor of the warehouse but, as money was short, the rest of the site would have to be developed with as little Council investment as possible. Converting the upper storeys into workshop units would enable an application to be made for Urban Programme funding for the building work involved, which could all be attributed to the industrial units. The County Architects designed a scheme which quantity surveyors from the City's Technical Services Department costed at £96,400. Under the Urban Programme the City Council would only have to pay 25% of the money themselves (£24,100), and with 10,500 sq.ft. of lettable space on the upper floors only a very modest rent would be required to generate an acceptable return on this investment. Furthermore, day-to-day oversight of the entire building would be no problem as Council staff would be permanently on duty in the museum.

Uses for the stables and office buildings which would complement the museum were sought. A place for refreshments was an obvious candidate, and this led to the idea of a pub and a restaurant which could not only serve visitors to the museum but would also draw in other users and activity to the site even at times when the museum was closed (figures 32 and 33). They would also generate rental income, and could be developed to a specification set by the Council, yet at no cost to the Council, through a 'design and build' contract (see p. 112).

Extensive environmental improvements were also necessary to make the site attractive to visitors. These included dredging the canal basin, relaying the courtyard, cleaning the front of the building and making a canalside path. Normally these would have been expensive, and would not in themselves have generated any return. However, the Planning Department controlled the City's Operation Clean-Up programme (see p. 113) and, by linking this with the MSC's Community Programme (see p. 98), was able to arrange for several environmental schemes to be carried out at the correct times in the development programme and at no apparent cost to the project. Cleaning out the canal basin itself was done by volunteers.

Because the development had been broken down into separate parts, each with its own funding mechanism, a sophisticated feasibility study was not required, the City Council was only investing a very small amount of its own money and this would be rapidly repaid by the rents.

NEGOTIATION STAGE

Raising the finance
For the warehouse conversion an Urban Programme grant of £96,400 spread over two years was approved. £28,000 was spent on environmental improvements under the DoE's Operation Clean-Up scheme. The setting up of the museum was covered under the Arts Department's normal operating budget. The development of the pub and restaurant was put out to competitive tender. Developers were offered a 50-year lease on the stables and office buildings at a reduced rent (52% of full market rent, after an initial period). In return the developer had to design and build a pub and restaurant which met a brief laid down by the Council. Whitbreads, one of the major brewers, made the best offer (initial rent: £12,000 per year) and their scheme designed by their in-house architects was of award winning standard. It even included a miniature brewery. The full cost of converting and fitting out their part of the scheme eventually came to £245,000.

Sources of finance

			£
Private Investment			245,000
Urban Programme	(75% DoE)		72,000
	(25% City of	Nottingham)	24,000
Operation Clean-Up	(75% DoE)		21,000
	(25% City of	Nottingham)	7,000
MSC – Salaries			Nil*
			£369,000

*So far as project was concerned

Maintaining flexibility

By dividing the scheme up into separate parts and in particular by making Whitbreads responsible for the most complicated part, the Council reduced its own risks considerably. Furthermore the warehouse conversion was done on a fixed price contract so that the costs would not normally exceed the amount of grant available. On the environmental improvement side there was considerable scope for flexibility, as the Planning Department itself controlled an Operation Clean-Up budget of about £800,000 per year of which about half was not tied to defined programmes. Furthermore the flexibility which this gave could be greatly increased by using the money in combination with an MSC workforce, and since the Council is a managing agent (see p. 113) for the MSC it is easy to organise such projects.

Finding appropriate professionals

Nottingham City Council had its own architects, quantity surveyors, lawyers and estates managers, and they were used to operating together as a team. This is a great advantage that a local authority has when undertaking developments. Whitbreads, too, had their own design and development departments. However both organisations could have used outside professionals if appropriate, and indeed architects from Nottinghamshire County Council did the design work for the museum. Fees for the in-house professionals were fully included in the project costings.

CONSTRUCTION STAGE

Using reliable contractors

Two main contractors were appointed, one for the warehouse conversion and one (by Whitbreads) for the conversion of the stables and office buildings. The environmental improvements were carried out by an MSC workforce. Thus there were at times three different workforces on one small site. However, experienced and well managed contractors were chosen and deliberate efforts were made to keep people and materials separate.

The work on the warehouse included putting in 2 staircases, a lift and all services. The aim was to provide basic, no frills space. There was also a substantial amount of work required by the fire regulations, mainly in ensuring adequate fire separation between the public and private uses on different floors.

Keeping control of time and money

Both contractors were responsible for the control of their own parts of the project. Any problems or cost over-runs were at their expense, not the Council's. The cost of the pub and restaurant did exceed the original estimates, but this was due to Whitbread's own decision to upgrade the specification and it did not alter their contract with the Council.

Project management

There was no overall project manager in charge of the building works. The appropriate architects oversaw the contractors' work. There were occasional co-ordination meetings, which included the representatives of Arts and Planning Departments, to ensure that all was going to plan.

MANAGEMENT STAGE

Marketing

Marketing presented few problems. The main users of the site were the museum and the pub and restaurant. They had been closely involved throughout the development. It was not difficult to find tenants for the industrial units. There were only 3 units to let. The rents were modest and the location conveniently close to the City centre. They were attractive to those who needed to store goods close to the shopping area. The City, the County and other tourist related bodies promoted the museum. Pubs rarely need much promotion and the miniature brewery proved quite an attraction.

Continuing management

The completed scheme was only 17,500 sq.ft. in size, and small schemes are usually expensive to manage. However in this case there was no problem. By their nature both a pub and a museum need responsible management on site all the time. The museum staff are also City Council employees and it is easy for them to oversee the site and deal with minor day-to-day problems as they arise. This saves the Technical Services Department much effort and expense, and ensures that the entire Canal Museum site is economically and well managed.

Notes

Operation Clean-up. A Department of the Environment scheme, now merged into the Urban Programme, under which grants were available for approved environmental improvement schemes in inner urban areas. In Nottingham, and in some other towns, the old name has been kept and applied to an overall strategic programme into which individual projects can be fitted, often at fairly short notice.

Project references

PROJECT ADDRESS	Nottingham Canal Museum, Canal Street, Nottingham NG1 7ET Telephone: 0602–598835
CONTACT	Jim Taylor, Nottingham City Council, The Guildhall, North Church Street, Nottingham NG1 4DB
PROJECT ARCHITECTS	Nottinghamshire County Architects, County Hall, West Bridgford, Nottingham NG2 7QJ Inn Design Services, Exchange Brewery, Bridge Street, Sheffield S3 8NL.

14 Pallion Residents Enterprises Ltd

Pallion Industrial Estate, Sunderland

Large post-war clothing factory, now re-used as a community centre with sports facilities and units for small firms. Developed by local residents' association using public finance and MSC work force.

GOOD PRACTICES HIGHLIGHTED

- Driving force
- Obtaining Public Support
- Formulating the Scheme
- Obtaining Local Authority Support
- Raising the Finance
- Using an MSC Workforce
- Keeping Control of Money

A trailblazing mixed use scheme combining community facilities and workspace for small firms in order to promote local employment especially for young people. This project was conceived and executed by a local residents' association as direct action to combat unemployment and to provide local leisure facilities. Great importance has been attached to local control and therefore to financial independence.

Key Facts

Original Building	Type:	Factory
	Construction:	Steel frame
	Date:	1947
	Size:	84,000 sq.ft.
	Storeys:	Mostly 1
	Location:	Industrial estate in residential area
	Configuration:	Rectangular
	Condition:	Vandalised
Concept	New Use:	Units/Sports/ Community/Pub
	Developer:	Residents' Association
	Approach:	Entrepreneurial
	Manager:	Project initiator
Finance	Public Sector:	£580,000
	Private Sector:	£117,000
Development	Tenure:	125-year lease
	Acquisition Cost:	£ 45,000
	Conversion Cost:	£652,000
	Date of Scheme:	1982 onwards
	Usable Area:	45,000 sq.ft.
	Cost per sq.ft. (gross):	£8.30 (1986 Equivalent: £8.40)*
	Cost per sq.ft. (net):	£15.40 (1986 Equivalent: £16.70)*
Result	No. of Units:	24 (increasing to 38) (plus sports hall, meeting rooms, pub)
	Employment:	120 (400 expected eventually)

*Adjusted for building cost inflation to approximate 1986 value

Figure 34: The factory during renovation, dark and basic

PROJECT SUMMARY

The building

The building is an 84,000 sq.ft. single storey former clothing factory on a small industrial estate in the Pallion district of Sunderland, about 1 mile from the town centre. The factory was built in 1947 and closed in 1981. It rapidly fell prey to vandals and glue sniffers from the surrounding housing estates, and its owners planned to demolish it (figure 34).

The problem

Sunderland, once a centre of shipbuilding and mining had suffered harsh economic decline. Youth unemployment in the Pallion district was around 70% and there were few opportunities for work. The area also lacked recreation facilities, making it difficult for young people to find anything constructive to do.

The scheme

Gordon Robson, a local councillor and a building foreman, wanted to take action. He called a public meeting which founded the Pallion Residents Association and set about planning a range of new uses for the building. The task was to persuade the Council to buy the lease, then to raise all the finance, establish a development organisation, convert the building using a local workforce and paying particular attention to training, and ensure that the new premises were well managed and generated sufficient income. All this Gordon Robson and the Residents Association did, using MSC workforces and mainly Urban Programme funding for materials.

The outcome

The project will take five years and not two as originally planned. But the building work has provided training for over 200 local people and is now substantially complete. All the completed industrial units and many of the offices are let (figure 35). The one remaining piece of work, developing a pub, has now been organised and funded. Income from it will ensure the independence and financial success of the project.

Organisation and management of the project

INCUBATION STAGE

Driving force

Gordon Robson was, and still is, the driving force that made the Pallion project happen. He was determined that something should be done about unemployment. He brought the Pallion Residents Association into existence and later became Project Manager of Pallion Residents Enterprises Ltd. (PRE). As project manager, he was in charge of the MSC workforce doing the

Figure 35: The type of workshop provided in the refurbished building

Figure 36: Special training for people with disabilities

conversion and he has remained on as manager to make sure that the project really does succeed. As a borough councillor he knew the system and had a wide range of contacts. As a former building foreman, he knew about building work and site management. As a local resident he knew what was needed in Pallion and he knew how to mobilise support for a good scheme.

Objectives

Gordon Robson's main objectives were to provide employment, training and community facilities. Thus the emphasis was not just on doing the conversion work, but more importantly on seeing that the new premises were in fact used and provided local employment. Furthermore the Pallion residents, once committed to this project, were determined to keep control of it in their own hands. Thus although the project grew out of a wish to re-use a particular building, it was the end-uses and not the building itself which were seen as important.

Obtaining public support

Gordon Robson had to move fast and he had to start from scratch. He learned in May 1982 that the clothing factory was going to be demolished in two months time. He immediately called a public meeting of local residents. Everyone agreed that a scheme to provide jobs and community facilities should be initiated. The Pallion Residents Association was formed, with a 4 person steering committee to oversee the scheme. Also four sub-committees involving over 100 local residents were formed to generate ideas on each of the main aspects of the scheme.

Formulating the scheme

Once strong local support had been demonstrated, immediate action was possible. A local architect and quantity surveyor looked over the 84,000 sq.ft. building and estimated that it would cost £5 per sq.ft. to convert using an MSC workforce. English Industrial Estates who owned the building shelved their demolition plans and gave the Association an 18-month 'licence to occupy'. The local Councils gave their backing. Tyne and Wear County Council gave the Association a £2,000 grant to make the building secure. Sunderland Borough Council agreed to buy the 125-year lease of the building at market value (£45,000) and rent it to the Association if funding could be arranged. They also gave an immediate £80,000 grant and a further loan in anticipation of the project receiving Urban Programme support in the following year.

Just as importantly the Borough Council seconded once of their staff, Chris Tillett, who knew Gordon Robson, to work full time on the project. His role was to liaise with all the public and private sector bodies involved, to establish the appropriate organisation, to develop its business plan and raise finance. This left Gordon Robson free to run the project. Chris Tillett had a friend in Coopers and Lybrand, a large accounting and business consulting firm, who persuaded one of the senior partners, Paul Southern, to attend a Residents Association meeting. He was able to give broad business and marketing advice. He strongly advised the Association to look for grants, rather than loan finance, so as to avoid burdening the project with interest charges. At his instigation Coopers and Lybrand prepared an outline feasibility study for the project which explained the proposed uses, small units, training, sports and community facilities and showed that the scheme could become financially self-supporting. This played an important part in persuading the various bodies to back the scheme.

In order to undertake the development a company called Pallion Residents Enterprises Ltd. (PRE) was formed in September 1982. Its shareholders had to live locally and its directors were drawn from the interested parties including, of course, the Residents Association.

Obtaining local authority support

As with all projects involving buildings and most projects seeking grants, the support of the local authorities is crucial, as Gordon Robson well knew. By being able to demonstrate that there was strong local support for his scheme he greatly increased the likehood of Council support, and in this case both the County Council and the Borough Council backed the scheme in full measure.

NEGOTIATION STAGE

Raising the finance

Since the financial year of 1982–83 was already in progress, PRE first tried to obtain an Urban Development Grant, which can be applied for at any time and does not have to be included in the local authority's annual Urban Programme submission. However, because there was no leveraging of private sector money, Urban Development Grant was refused. Urban Programme funding was therefore applied for, but for the financial year starting in April 1983, and £354,000 was approved.

Meanwhile Gordon Robson immediately set about starting a Manpower Services Commission (MSC) project (see p. 113) through Sunderland Borough Council. As youth unemployment was the great problem he used the Youth Opportunities Programme (YOP) which was shortly replaced by the Youth Training Scheme (YTS) (see p. 105). Being a builder, he was able to act as an MSC supervisor himself. By January 1983 there were 32 trainees and 5 supervisors on the site, by the following November, when the project became a YTS managing agent in its own right, there were 50 trainees and 8 supervisors. The total cost of the building works to the project has only been around £650,000 so far, because the workforce has effectively been free. A normal contractor, using paid labour, would have charged about £1.5 million for the same work. The immense hidden contribution of the MSC to the scheme should not be overlooked.

Other funding was not easy to obtain, but the Residents Association was a forceful group with a good cause. Having a vicar on the steering committee reinforced this image. In the end £40,000 was raised from the Sports Council for the recreational facilities, a further £44,000 came from the County Council to provide sophisticated telephone equipment. £23,000 was raised from the European Regional Development Fund to equip a special training workshop for disabled people (figure 36). The EEC provided one half of this grant and Sunderland Borough Council the other half. In addition local firms donated equipment worth £150,000 for this training workshop and much free advice, and the National Council for Voluntary Organisations (NCVO) gave a small grant for management development. Later, for the conversion of part of the building into a pub a brewery provided a loan of £100,000. Thus the project obtained support from a wide range of sources.

Maintaining financial flexibility

Schemes which rely heavily on public funding often lack flexibility, and so the cash implications of events have to be carefully watched. In this case, Coopers and Lybrand's advised PRE to register for VAT as soon as possible in order to be able to reclaim the tax that was going to be charged on all the materials and supplies it bought, and which it is easy to forget to allow for. They also warned that grants can sometimes be treated as income by the Inland Revenue and taxed if there is not sufficient expenditure to set against them in any financial year. While the tax might be recoverable in a later year, the fact that it had to be paid out initially could lead to an unexpected cash crisis.

In spite of careful planning, the project did run into financial difficulties. The conversion work, using MSC workforces, took much longer than originally planned, delaying the anticipated income. A private developer who had been expected to refurbish one part of the building pulled out suddenly, leaving PRE with extra work which it had not budgetted for. Furthermore the Urban Programme grant application had been based on a conversion cost of £5.50 per sq.ft., the maximum that the Borough Council would contemplate, whereas the architect now thought that £7.50 would be required. However, sensing that the Council had reached their limit, Gordon Robson decided to accept the lower figure and get on with the work, rather than to jeopardize the whole project. Eventually, of course, a substantial deficit occurred. Fortunately, however, relations with the local authorities were so good that the County Council and the Borough Council agreed to pay an extra £59,500 each and so provide the flexibility which the scheme so desperately needed.

104

CONSTRUCTION STAGE

Project management

Gordon Robson has been the project manager throughout. He is answerable to PRE's Board of Directors, which ensures that there is genuine local control. However it is Gordon Robson's deep and continuing commitment to the project and its end-uses that has ensured its success. It has also been an advantage that he has been able to lead the building team himself as well as organising the project as a whole. If there is a problem on or off the site he can go and sort it out, and there is no question of the scheme drifting off course while he is involved in all aspects of it.

Sources of finance

	£
Urban Programme (75% DoE)	265,500
(25% Sunderland)	88,500
Tyne and Wear County Council Grant	44,000
Sports Council Grant	40,000
ERDF (50% EEC)	11,500
(50% Sunderland)	11,500
Donations from Local Firms	15,000
NCVO Management Development Grant	2,000
Brewery Loan	100,000
Additional Funding	
– Sunderland	59,500
– Tyne and Wear	59,500
MSC – Salaries	Nil*
	£697,000

*So far as project as concerned

Using an MSC workforce

From the outset it was the intention to use an MSC workforce on the Pallion project. Lack of training was seen as one reason why young people could not get jobs. The building work required to convert the factory could be used to train young people in building skills, and this in itself became an important part of the project. PRE became a managing agent for a 50 place YTS scheme. It was easily able to recruit local young people and, in conjunction with the MSC, a training programme was worked out based on 6 'learning packages' from which each individual could choose a skill to learn. The training took much longer and required much more energy to organise than originally envisaged, but otherwise there were no major difficulties. As training was seen as important in its own right the slower progress was acceptable. Most of the conversion work was done very satisfactorily by the trainees, working under their experienced supervisors, but a few jobs, such as asbestos clearing and electrical works, required special skills. These were provided through a Community Programme scheme, also paid for by the MSC but using an older and more experienced workforce (see p. 113).

Not only was the building work done at a much lower cost to the project than would otherwise have been possible, but also the quality of the training provided was so good that over a third of the trainees found permanent local jobs before their period of training was finished. This was a far higher level than any other construction training project in the region obtained.

Keeping control of money

As PRE had no experience of handling large sums of money and no proper organisation for doing so, a system was devised with the help of Sunderland Borough Council whereby the Council held all money on behalf of PRE. It even kept the balances on deposit to earn interest. All payments were approved by an authorised member of PRE, by the Quantity Surveyor, and by Sunderland's Industrial Development Officer before being paid by Treasurer's Department. Thus the PRE did not handle the money. This was a rather cumbersome system but it did work, even on a large scheme, and there was never any fear of money going astray due to inexperience in managing it. If the local authority had not been willing to act in this way a similar system could have been arranged through some other responsible body.

MANAGEMENT STAGE

Marketing

The Pallion project has not lacked publicity. It is unique as a local community scheme and has therefore attracted television, radio and press coverage. This made it easier to get outside advice and help, when needed, from the very best sources. It has also meant that there has been substantial interest in the workspaces without the need to do any marketing. There is in fact a waiting list for the units and they are occupied as soon as they become available.

Continuing management

For the time being Gordon Robson remains in charge of the project and the building management, although other people also play a part in the management of the different facilities (e.g. catering, sports). But ultimately the residents of the Pallion district are in control. This is their project, helping to revive their area, and they want to see that it keeps on doing just that.

Notes

Youth Training Scheme (YTS). An MSC scheme to encourage employers to provide work experience and training for 16 and 17 year old school leavers for a period of up to 2 years. A managing agent is responsible for organising a complete programme for a number of trainees. The MSC pays a training allowance for each trainee and contributes towards the employer's overheads and training costs.

Project references

PROJECT ADDRESS	Pallion Residents Enterprises Ltd., Pallion Industrial Estate, Roper Street, Sunderland SR4 6SN Telephone: 0783–655959
CONTACT	Gordon Robson
PROJECT ARCHITECTS	Anthony Watson, The Esplanade, Sunderland SR2 7BQ.

Appendices

A Some useful references

Those wishing to know more about specific aspects of the conversion and re-use of old industrial and commercial buildings might find the following publications useful. Those which are referred to in the text are numbered accordingly.

(1) Jackson A. et al. *Managing Workspaces: Case Studies of Good Practice in Urban Regeneration* (HMSO, 1987)

(2) Cantacuzino, S. *New Uses for Old Buildings* (Architectural Press, 1975)

(3) Hanna, M. and Binney M. *Preservation Pays – Tourism and the economic benefits of conserving historic buildings* (SAVE, undated)

(4) URBED *Space to Work: Report to the Hackney/Islington/ DoE Partnership* (URBED, 1980)

(5) Rock, D. *The Grassroots Developers – a handbook for Town Development Trusts* (RIBA Conference Fund, 1980)

(6) Cadman, D. and Austin-Crowe, L. *Property Development* (Spon, 1983)

(7) *Commercial Property Development ('The Pilcher Report)* (HMSO, 1975)

(8) Landry, C. et al. *What a Way to Run a Railroad* (Comedia, 1975)

(9) URBED *Recycling Industrial Buildings* (Capital Planning Information, 1981)

(10) Norton, M. ed. *Raising Money from Government* (Directory of Social Change, 1985)

(11) Eley, P. and Worthington, J. *Industrial Rehabilitation – the use of redundant buildings for small enterprises* (The Architectural Press, 1984)

(12) Green, H. and Foley, P. *Redundant Space – A Productive Asset: converting property for small business use* (Harper and Row, 1986)

(13) *Financial Resources for Economic Development* (The Planning Exchange)

(14) DoE *Finding Profitable Uses for New Buildings: The Scope for Using Government Grants* (DoE, 1984)

(15) Martinos, H. *Workspace Developments for Small Businesses* (The Planning Exchange, 1985)

(16) Davidson, A. *Grants from Europe* (NCVO, 1984)

(17) Green, R. *The Architects Guide to Running a Job* (Architectural Press, 1986)

(18) English Heritage, Forthcoming series of reference sources for potential developers of redundant buildings (Due for publication in 1987)

(19) Catt, R. and Catt, S. *The Conversion, Improvement and Extension of Buildings* (Estates Gazette, 1981)

(20) DoE Audit Inspectorate *Control of Capital Projects* (HMSO, 1982)

(21) R. Tym and Partners *Mills in the 80's* (Report to Greater Manchester Council and West Yorkshire County Council, 1984)

Scottish Civic Trust *New Uses for Older Buildings in Scotland – a manual of practical encouragement* (Edinburgh HMSO, 1981)

British Tourist Authority *Britain's Historic Buildings – a policy for their future use* (BTA, 1981)

Marsh, P. *The Refurbishment of Commercial and Industrial Buildings* (Construction Press, 1983)

Stephenson, J. and Rawson, J. *Community Buildings Project Pack* (NCVO, 1983)

Royal Borough of Kensington and Chelsea *Urban Conservation and Historic Buildings – a guide to the legislation* (The Architectural Press, 1984)

Local Economic Development Information Service (The Planning Exchange, Glasgow, Continuing Series)

B Statistics on conversions
of industrial and commercial buildings in Britain

The following table, drawn from the files of the Re-use of Industrial Buildings Service (RIBS)*, categorises 400 conversion schemes which have been carried out in Britain in the past few years. The table is not exhaustive but it indicates that:–

- over half the schemes were carried out by private developers

- most of the buildings were originally warehouses or factories

- workspace (small units) is the most common new use, but the range of new uses is very wide.

Explanation of terms
The terms used to categorise projects are based on those used by the Montagu Committee (a working party set up in 1979 by the Historic Buildings Council for England and the British Tourist Authority to look at possible alternative uses for historic buildings). The following explanations may be useful:

Working Community	:	buildings with many occupants sharing common services and reception facilities
Mixed Use	:	buildings with uses which span different categories
Other Buildings	:	include stables, granaries, garages, maltings, pumping stations, work houses, etc.

Note: Public buildings are not included in these statistics

*Re-used of industrial buildings service (RIBS): Provides community groups and voluntary associations with information, advice and in some cases technical aid in putting together schemes for re-using redundant industrial and commercial buildings. It was established in 1982 with 50% grant aid under the Department of the Environment's Urban Initiatives Fund and is operated by URBED, 99 Southwark Street, London SE1.

Type of new use	Type of developer				Type of building						%
	Private	Voluntary	Local Authority	Trust	Factory	Ware-house	Mill	Railway Building	Other	Total	
Workspace											
Industrial Units	20	–	12	8	22	7	6	2	3	40	10.0%
Working Communities	11	–	2	5	11	4	–	–	3	18	4.5%
Craft Workshops	6	1	3	1	3	6	–	–	2	11	2.75%
Small Offices	34	–	6	–	12	15	8	–	5	40	10.0%
Design Studios	10	–	–	5	3	9	1	–	2	15	3.75%
Technology Based Industry	5	–	4	2	6	1	2	1	1	11	2.75%
Training Workshops	–	–	4	1	1	1	1	1	1	5	1.25%
Community Workshops	–	3	–	1	1	1	–	–	2	4	1.0 %
Various	24	–	5	5	16	8	4	1	5	34	8.5 %
Workspace – Total	110	4	36	28	75	52	22	5	24	178	44.5%
Leisure/retail											
Shops/Market Stalls Warehouses	10	–	2	–	2	5	2	2	1	12	3.0 %
Refreshment Facilities	5	–	–	1	–	1	1	3	1	6	1.5 %
Hotel & Holiday Accommodation	7	–	1	–	1	3	2	1	1	8	2.0 %
Entertainment Facilities	6	–	1	5	–	4	1	2	5	12	3.0 %
Social Recreation Facilities	4	4	4	11	3	9	3	–	8	23	5.75%
Sports Facilities	3	1	4	–	1	2	–	1	4	8	2.0 %
Library/Education	4	2	2	2	–	1	4	2	3	10	2.5 %
Museums	13	–	12	24	7	7	18	7	10	49	12.25%
Leisure-retail Total	52	7	26	43	14	32	31	18	33	128	32.9 %
Housing											
Public Housing	1	–	4	2	3	3	1	–	–	7	1.75%
Private Housing	23	–	1	6	6	11	7	–	6	30	7.5 %
Housing Total	24	–	5	8	9	14	8	–	6	37	9.25%
Mixed Use											
Multiple Building	5	1	5	7	3	7	4	–	4	18	4.5 %
Residence/Workspace	5	–	1	–	2	1	1	–	2	6	1.5 %
Community/ Commercial Mixed Use	4	3	5	4	5	6	2	1	2	16	4.0 %
Commercial Mixed Use	11	–	3	3	3	7	4	–	3	17	
Mixed Use Total	25	4	14	14	13	21	11	1	11	57	4.25%
TOTAL	211	15	81	93	111	119	72	24	74	400	100.00
%	52.75	3.75	20.25	23.25	27.75	29.75	18.0	6.0	18.5	100%	

C Explanation of jargon

Every effort has been made to avoid jargon. However, some people may not be familiar with a few of the terms that appear in the case studies. These are explained in the case study notes and are repeated here in alphabetical order for easy reference.

Co-operatives. A workers' co-operative is a business which is owned and controlled by all those who work in it. Decisions are made on the principle that every worker has one vote and only workers vote. The profits made belong to the business generally and not to individuals within it.

Design and build contract. A type of building contract under which the contractor takes responsibility not only for the construction work but also for its design and specification. The developer prepares a performance specification which sets out the precise requirements for the building and the contractor commits to meeting those requirements, usually at a fixed price. The contractor employs the architect and takes a substantial share of the development risk (and is likely to make allowance for this in the price).

Fair rent. A controlled rent (for housing) set by a local authority Rent Officer in order to stop private landlords overcharging their tenants. Most tenants in private housing have the legal right to apply for a fair rent, which is likely to be below the free market rent. It is a condition of the DoE's Improvement Grants that only fair rents are charged for at least the first five years if a grant aided property is let.

Financial institutions groups (FIG). A group of 26 leading financial institutions which were invited by the Secretary of State for the Environment to send a representative to visit Liverpool with him in the Summer of 1981 to learn about inner city problems. During the next year they put forward ideas and initiatives to help promote urban regeneration.

Housing association. A non-profit organisation run by a voluntary committee to provide housing for the benefit of the community or, in some cases, for the benefit of its members. Many housing associations provide housing let at fair (controlled) rents. Some also provide housing for purchase. To be eligible to receive public funding under the Housing Act 1974 associations must be registered with, and supervised by, the Housing Corporation.

Index-linked mortgage. A rare type of mortgage which has a low rate of interest, say 4% per year, but the amount of capital which is repaid each year over the life of the loan increases in line with inflation. The effect of this is that the annual repayments start low but increase over time. But, of course, the rental income from which the mortgage repayments have to come, should also increase over time.

Industrial and provident society (IPS). A non-profit organisation registered with the Registrar of Friendly Societies and incorporated under the Industrial and Provident Societies Act 1965, which must be either a bona fide co-operative or a business run for community benefit. Unlike an unincorporated friendly society, an IPS has limited liability which means that those who run it are not personally liable for its debts if things go wrong. Housing Associations are usually constituted this way.

JCT contract. The most generally used form of contract for building work, under which the developer is responsible for the design, specification and supervision of the work and the contractor for carrying out the work as specified. It has standard clauses covering how payments are to be made, what happens (and who bears the costs) when changes occur, and many other eventualities.

Listed buildings. Buildings of special architectural or historic interest are listed by the Historic Buildings Division of the DoE, and formal Listed Building Consent is required before any alteration, extension or demolition can take place. The list is divided into three categories:

Grade I	Buildings of National Importance.
Grade II*	Particularly Important Buildings in Grade II
Grade II	Buildings of Special Architectural or Historic Interest

There are about 300,000 listed buildings in England, but fewer than 6,000 are Grade I.

Local enterprise agency. A local organisation which promotes new enterprise and local economic development in its area, usually sponsored by the local authority in partnership with major local firms, the Chamber of Commerce and banks. There are now approximately 250 Enterprise Agencies in Britain. Business in the Community, 277a City Road, London EC1 is the national organisation which promotes Local Enterprise Agencies.

The London Small Business Property Trust. LSBPT was formed in 1982 by CIPFA Services Ltd., Granby Hunter and URBED. It is a unit trust aimed at attracting local authority pension funds to invest in property let to small businesses in their areas. At the same time it fills a funding gap by allowing those who develop small units to realise their investment. So far it has invested approximately £10 million, all in the London area.

Management fee contract. A way of organising a building contract under which an outside project manager is brought in to supervise the contractors or subcontractors and ensure that they carry out the work as specified on time and within budget. The project manager takes a fee but relieves the developer, and their professional team, of direct responsibility for managing the building works.

Manpower Services Commission (MSC). A government agency with responsibility for training and employment creation. The Community Programme is a temporary employment scheme under which the MSC pays wages and other costs, up to set limits, to enable the long term unemployed to work on community projects that would not otherwise be done. A managing agent administers a number of projects under a contract with the MSC.

Operation Clean-Up. A Department of the Environment scheme, now merged into the Urban Programme, under which grants were available for approved environmental improvement schemes in inner urban areas. In Nottingham, and in some other towns, the old name has been kept and applied to an overall strategic programme into which individual projects can be fitted, often at fairly short notice.

Rating of partially occupied buildings. Since April 1984 empty industrial buildings have been exempt from rates. But once any space is used the whole is liable for full rates. Care must therefore to taken to ensure that the parts of a large building that are capable of being occupied separately are rated separately (by the Inland Revenue's Valuation Officer), so that the exemption can be claimed on the parts which are not occupied.

Royal Institute of British Architects (RIBA). The professional body for architects in Britain, it acts as a source of information for those new to property conversion who need to be put in touch with local architects with relevant experience. Contact either the Community Architecture Department, or the Client Advisory Service, 66 Portland Place, London W1 (01–580 5533).

Trust. A body which is responsible for managing money given to it for a specified purpose. It is often used in the name of organisations to imply that their aim is public, rather than private, benefit. A Trust undertaking property development is often constituted as a Company Limited by Guarantee, which has no shareholders and may not distribute profits, yet the individuals running it are not personally liable for its debts if things go wrong.

Youth Training Scheme (YTS). An MSC scheme to encourage employers to provide work experience and training for 16 and 17 year old school leavers for a period of up to 2 years. A managing agent is responsible for organising a complete programme for a number of trainees. The MSC pays a training allowance for each trainee and contributes towards the employer's overheads and training costs.

D Urban Programme Authorities

The following local authority districts were invited to prepare Inner Area Programmes for Urban Programme funding in 1987/88.

Barnsley	Liverpool
Birmingham	Manchester
Blackburn	Middlesbrough
Bolton	Newham
Bradford	Nottingham
Brent	Newcastle
Bristol	North Tyneside
Burnley	Oldham
Coventry	Preston
Derby	Plymouth
Doncaster	Rochdale
Dudley	Rotherham
Gateshead	Salford
Greenwich	Sandwell
Hackney	Sefton
Halton	Sheffield
Hammersmith & Fulham	Southwark
Haringey	South Tyneside
Hartlepool	St. Helens
Islington	Stockton on Tees
Kensington & Chelsea	Sunderland
Kingston upon Hull	Tower Hamlets
Kirklees	Walsall
Knowsley	Wandsworth
Langbaurgh	Wigan
Lambeth	Wirral
Leeds	Wolverhampton
Leicester	Wrekin
Lewisham	

E Acknowledgements

URBED would like to thank the following people for their contributions to this handbook and the case studies. Their information and assistance has been invaluable.

J. Barr
Teresa Bednall
Jim Beeston
Roderick Begg
Ian Bennett
Colin Bishop
Graham Bourne
Alain Bouvie
Mr. Boyd
Malcolm Brumwell
Ian Burnet
Tony Byrne
David Chapman
W. Chapman
Vivian Church
John Collins
Mike Crook
Alan Dale
Francis Daly
Tony Eade
Margaret Elliot
Reg Elmer
Alf Everest
Mike Fenton
Michael Franklin
Bill Fulford
Larry Gould
Ernest Hall
Jeremy Hall
John Haslam
Ian Holden
Ron Howarth
Esther Jennings
Jim Johnson
Peter Kelly
Janet Keighley
Denise Kirwan
Tom Laurie

Eric Lee
Steve Lloyd
Nick Mahoney
Martin Mayer
Eleanor McAllister
Brian McInally
Roger Mortimer
Hugh O'Donnell
Roger O'Hare
David Parry
Philip Perry
Niall Phillips
Steve Pinhay
Mike Pindar
Mr. Power
Darren Ratcliffe
Eric Reynolds
Gordon Robson
Jim Ross
Robert Seager
Graham Shaylor
Oliver Shirley
David Simmons
Peter Soulder
Kevin Sheridan
Mike Short
Paul Smith
Paul Southern
Jim Taylor
Chris Tillett
Gary Townsend
Neil Walker
Anthony Watson
Peter Wheeler
Peter White
Angela Wilson
Simon Woodhurst
John Worthington

Printed in the United Kingdom for Her Majesty's Stationery Office
Dd.239043. C20. 7/87. 3936. 12521